THE

ULTIMATE

SEARCH

BOOK

U.S. Adoption, Genealogy
& Other Search Secrets

by

Lori Carangelo

Access Press

Copyright 2021 and forward by Lori Carangelo
Sixth Edition, Revised and Updated

Previous publishers, The Ultimate Search Book - U.S. Editions:
2018 edition, ISBN 978-0-942605-42-6, Access Press
2015 edition, ISBN 978-0-8063-5729-4 , Clearfield Company for Genealogical Publishing
2013 edition, ISBN 0-942605-26-8, Access Press
2012 edition, ISBN 0-942605-12-8, Access Press
1997 edition, ISBN 0-942605-00-4, Garlic Press

Previous publishers, The Ultimate Search Book - Worldwide Editions:
2018 edition – ISBN 978-0-942605-40-2, Access Press
2011 edition - ISBN 978-0-9063-5515-3, Clearfield Company
2000-2002 editions - ISBN 0-87047-121-X, Schenkman Books Inc.
1998-1999 editions - ISBN 1-877-677-85-8, Heritage Quest

Library of Congress CIP 96-86255

Printed in the United States of America

ISBN: 978-0-942605-69-3

This book is dedicated to all who have had to endure
"impossible" searches for answers to
"Who am I?" and *"Is my child alive and well?"*

`````````````````````````

*155-million Americans Affected by Secrecy of Vital Records
(almost half of the United States population of 329-million in 2019)

13,000,000
Maternal
Grandparents

13,000,000
Maternal
Grandparents

7,000,000
Birthmothers

7,000,000
Adoptive
Mothers

13,000,000
Maternal
Aunts & Uncles

13,000,000
Maternal
Aunts & Uncles

13,000,000
Paternal
Grandparents

7,000,000
Birthfathers

7,000,000
Adoptive
Fathers

13,000,000
Paternal
Grandparents

13,000,000
Paternal
Aunts & Uncles

13,000,000
Paternal
Aunts & Uncles

8,000,000
Birth Siblings

8,000,000
Birth Siblings

7,000,000
Adoptees

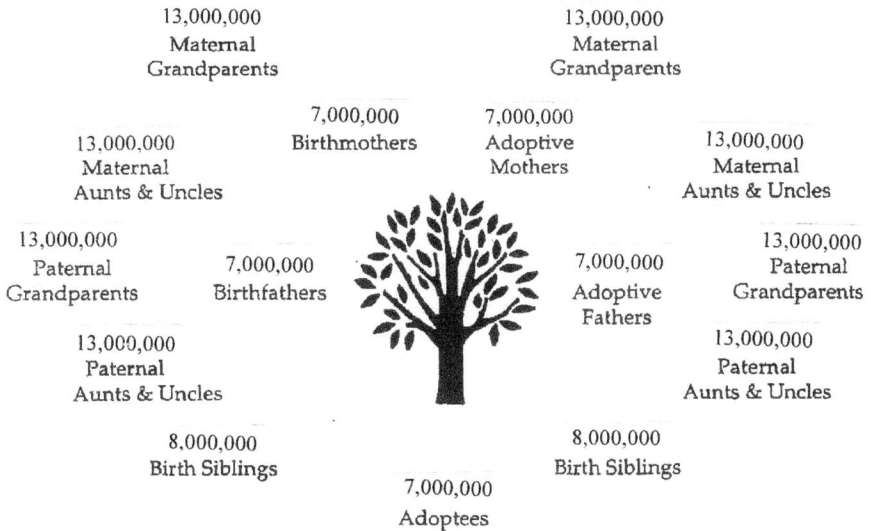
`````````````````````````

DISCLAIMER

The U.S. and Worldwide Editions of *The Ultimate Search Book* have had several updated editions over the past two decades to enable completion of searches at little or no expense. Both volunteer "search angels" and paid search businesses, as well as other resources, are listed for information purposes, not intended as endorsement by the author or publisher of any individual or group. Groups online that welcome adoptees or birthparents or both can be especially *supportive*. Emails, website addresses (URLs) and phone numbers provided in this book, deemed reliable at the time of publication, are subject to change over time. However many of the mentioned individuals, groups and entities may also have a Facebook page that enable messaging via "Friending."

State adoption disclosure laws have been amended over the years and there may be proposed legislation or an amendment in effect after this book's publication. For example: Connecticut's *current* law under SB 972 limits access to adult adoptees whose adoptions were finalized *on or after October 1, 1983*. But in 2021, Connecticut Bill HB 6105 seeks to expand access to birth certificates for adopted persons age 18 and older, *and their adult children or grandchildren, regardless of the adoptee's date of birth*, to obtain an uncertified copy of the adoptee's original birth certificate on request. Follow the bill's progress at https://legiscan.com/CT/bill/HB06105/2021

The Bibliography in this book includes books for further reading that are not only search-related but also share adoptee/birthparent *experiences*.

Find your family, find yourself. Wishing all a speedy and rewarding search.

~The Author

Contents

1

"A right is not a right in America, unless it is enjoyed by all Americans."
-Archibald Cox, Special Watergate Prosecutor

Preface

DNA Testing Can Greatly Shortcut or Just Begin A Search

Almost everyone has a friend or relative whose absence has left a hole in their heart and unanswered questions. They are seeking information and may like to reconnect with them. For people who were adopted at birth or in childhood, or were donor conceived, as well as for parents who had to relinquish a child to adoption, secrecy about these family separations is still cruelly imposed by state law. Sealing of birth records and creation of "amended" (falsified) birth certificates was intended to prevent adoptees, even in adulthood, from having knowledge of, or access to, their biological relatives so profoundly connected to their own sense of self – their own identity. Even in modern "open," "semi-open" and stepparent adoptions, statutory falsification and sealing of birth records, broken promises, and unenforceable visitation agreements can also result in grief from loss and betrayal.

This book not only details DNA and genealogical mapping but also provides options for *locating* the "missing piece" of your puzzle - *with or without DNA testing.*

DNA testing has shortcut many family searches, particularly for someone whose identity is unknown due to adoption, IF a biologically related cousin, sibling, parent or other relative has *also* provided DNA to one or all of the 3 recommended DNA testing services for a "match" to result. They are **23&me.com** (when DNA results are then uploaded to **GenMatch.com**), **AncestryDNA.com**, and **FamilyTreeDNA.com)**; it is recommended that all 3 testing services be utilized. A "match" to a biological relative, such as a second cousin, then entails a genealogical search to narrow down closer relatives and target relative(s) who then need to be *located.*

The Ultimate Search Book results from the 20,000 family searches and reunions in 20 years that the author and her national network, AMERICANS FOR OPEN RECORDS (AmFOR) – (https://www.facebook.com/AmFOR.net/) helped facilitate, without fees, by networking nationwide and worldwide. Over time, she became privy to "insider" search secrets of professional investigators and amateur searchers, and learned how to legally circumvent the system via public records, and developed sources similarly motivated to interpret restrictive laws more broadly and provide the "missing pieces" – the missing knowledge and the people who were lost or made to "disappear" -- in order to answer lifelong questions such as *"Who am I?* and *"Is my child alive and well?"*

"Brains and wits will beat huge spending ten times out of ten."

-Ross Perot

Chapter 1:
SEARCH BASICS - 50 Search Tips for Starters

1. BEGIN WITH A LIST of all known names, dates, places related to your search. Keep notes on what you've tried to avoid duplicating your efforts. Place your list and any notes, however short, in a folder to which you can add any additional notes and documents as they are acquired.

2. LAST NAME SEARCHES: FIRST CHECK THE OBVIOUS. Sometimes the easiest or most obvious means of finding someone is overlooked. A friend of mine had always wanted to find her father who she never knew. His name was on her birth certificate along with his last known address. Within 2 minutes, the online directory at WhitePages.com produced her father's current address and phone number at no charge. However, such information on WhitePages.com is no longer free. And information on any "people search" website will only be as current as it was when posted. So if you're looking for someone who is 45 years old today, but you find same name listings for individuals who are 42 to 44, they can be considered "possibles" when coupled with additional known information. Ways to obtain information online without cost (such as via Facebook and via "Search Angels") is prioritized in this book because paying doesn't necessarily shortcut a search. Intellius.com, BeenVerified.com, PeopleSearch.com and others offering information for a fee but may not work if a common name is researched with no other identifiers such as age or date of birth, and there's no guarantee as to how current the information may be.

3. REVERSE LOOKUPS, NO NAME/BIRTH DATE ONLY SEARCHES. Search Gateway, at searchgateway.com (aka page name Freeality.com, once totally free, now links to mostly fee-based services, but it's an all-in-one search resource for name, address, phone, email, website lookups. PeopleFinders.com provides searches by name, while DOBSEARCH.com provides names of people with same date of birth, along with other helpful identifiers. (See also Search Tip #6: "YEARBOOKS FOR FIRST NAME/NO NAME SEARCHES, AND CHILD UNDER 18; and also Search Tip #25: "FIRST NAME/AGE ONLY SEARCHES.")

4. FACEBOOK. If you know the name of the person you seek but they have an unlisted phone number and it's not on WhitePages.com, 411.com, or other online directories, and the name is not too common, check to see if they are on Facebook. Facebook has over a billion members. By registering at Facebook.com you can also post information about yourself and/or about the person you seek, add photos, even a video, and maintain various levels of privacy according to your choice of settings, and still search and contact members via the messaging option by sending them a "Friend" request. You can also post information and photos in Facebook Newsfeeds that can be seen by Friends you add, as well as their Friends. Facebook pages may show their names and photos as well as where they've been – home towns, schools, affiliations, employment or business, family members, political and social interests, etc.

5. GOOGLE SEARCH. You may "get lucky" using Google.com by using the persons name or "key words." If a common name such as "Johnson," use "Johnson" together with other identifiers such as birth date and/or place or city where last known, or their profession. The more you know about the person before you begin — the easier it will be to whittle down same-name listings. You may bring up the person's photo, their own web page, their genealogy, a published post or comment they made on a chat site, an public obituary or an article written by or about the person.

6. YEARBOOKS FOR "FIRST NAME/NO NAME SEARCHES." Do you know their probable age or year of birth and last known location? If so, then you can guesstimate the year they graduated high school (usually the year they were 18), determine names of high schools in the area, and check the graduating classes for the year at Classmates.com and Reunions.com. You need to "join" these sites to search them. But if you are searching for an unknown parent, adoptee, sibling or other relative, these sites may display donated high school yearbooks for the year needed. Women's maiden names change from marriage but even if you don't know the current name you might discover the name if you find a photo with matching first name and family resemblance.

7. NAME CHANGE FROM MARRIAGE, DIVORCE, ADOPTION. In cases of marriage, divorce, re-marriage, and adoption, the person you seek will usually have had a name change, whether by choice or by law. While step-children in step-parent adoptions generally know who their re-married or divorced parents are, children of non-relative or stranger adoptions usually grow up not knowing who their biological parents are.

8. BIRTH CERTIFICATES. The birth certificate is the "breeder" document establishing a person's identity in any country, and is the basis for issuance of a passport, driver's license, Social Security Card, etc. The Addendum section contains images of some of the many types of birth certificates issued in the United States, as there is *no uniform document nationwide*. An individual may have several kinds -- Hospital Issued, City or County Issued; State Issued, Privately Issued, Church Issued/Baptismal, a Delayed Record, Certified Original or an Amended (Falsified) Birth Certificate, or Foreign Birth Certificate. In most states, even adult adoptees are not permitted to have a copy of their original (true) birth certificates, regardless whether it was an open, semi-open or closed adoption but check the state law for adult adoptee access to their original birth certificate in which the adoption was *finalized* (see pages 28-29 in this book). Your adopter(s) most likely have never been given much information nor *identifying* documents, depending on whether they met the biological mother before the adoption, or whether the adoption was facilitated decades ago when the biological parents *may have been named on certain documents*. But if you were adopted and want to know about or meet your biological family, begin by asking your adopter(s) for whatever information and documents they may have – including the Petition To Adopt, Final Decree of Adoption, and your birth certificate. A checklist in Chapter 2 will explain what you can do to obtain such records from the court of jurisdiction and/or adoption agency, by state, for the state in which your adoption was finalized. Varying types of disclosure may be available to a biological parent or sibling, post-adoption. Every state now has a provision for obtaining **at least non-identifying background information** from both the court and agency.

A birth certificate is also required to register a child in school, to enter the military, or to obtain a passport. In cases of stolen children and black market adoptees, the person may discover later in life that he or she has NO birth certificate. Only a few states currently permit adult adoptees to obtain their original birth certificate simply by requesting it with ID. Chapter 2: "With or Without a Name," includes a chart that details who may contact whom and how in each state – the state in which the adoption was finalized – and also details "how to search." An adopted person's birth certificate – which will most likely be the "amended" version not available from your local vital records office, only from the central office at the state's capital - names the adopters as the parents on day of birth. But also the information may be limited depending on whether a state issues multiple forms of the same document – for instance, a "long form" birth certificate which would have the most detail, a "short form," or, as in Connecticut, a coupon sized certificate. The long form may indicate the most information, such as the hospital where the adoptee was born. The adoptee's "original" birth certificate would have been sealed (placed in a locked or restricted file) by the court when the adoption was finalized, and even if subsequently released by court order, it would only be available from the state capital office of vital records. Both the original and amended birth certificates usually bear the same Registration Number.

Although a birth certificate may be sealed (access restricted) by court order for a number of reasons, it's most often done upon finalization of an adoption via a Final Decree of Adoption – usually within one year from the Petition to Adopt and placement of the child in his adoptive home. The original record remains in the court's file for life, becoming "non-existent" in law, even if subsequently released by court order, and a new "Amended" (falsified) birth certificate is then issued which replaces the names the child's biological parents with the adopter(s) names as if they were the parent(s) on the child's date of birth. Other "identifying" information may be omitted on the Amended version, including the name of the hospital and attending physician. The date and time of birth are usually the same, unless it was an illegal black market (or gray market, meaning questionable) adoption with false original or severely altered "amended" birth certificates.

Although there are no uniform state issued birth certificates, and therefore it is difficult to spot a forgery, the United States uses a common system of **state issued Birth Certificate Registration numbers** as result of an agreement among the states decades ago and the adoptee's falsified version retains the same recording numbers as the original birth certificate, except that a state birth number will not appear on a birth certificate issued by a county registrar. County registrars use county registrar file numbers. A mis-match will alert a Passport Clerk to confiscate the birth record as fraudulent or generate a request for the original birth certificate.

THE BIRTH CERTIFICATE NUMBERING SYSTEM

Example: Birth Certificate Registration Number 1-34-75-123456:
First digit is always "1"
Next 2 digits represent State of birth: "34" is Ohio
Next 2 digits represent year of birth: "75" is 1975
Last 6 digits are the State File Number, a random sequential number

The United States is unique among nations because our birth recording system is highly decentralized and is done on many levels – hospital, county and state. In some states, authorities have attempted to make it more difficult for a "new identity" seeker to obtain state maintained birth records. But often, in these same states, other types of birth records may be equally acceptable,

HOSPITAL BIRTH CERTIFICATE. Today, most people were born in hospitals but it is certainly not universal. In some states, over half of all births occurred outside hospitals. When a baby is born in a hospital, the attending physician or nurse fills out a short form indicating the time, sex and type of birth. Once out of the recovery room, the physician completes the hospital's standard birth certificate form which will have the name and location of the hospital, the name of the attending physician and some basic information, usually provided by the mother – including the parents' names and their ages at time of the birth, the baby's name, sex and time of birth, and perhaps the parents' race and n u m b e r of previous births. No two births are ever recorded at the exact same hour and minute at the same hospital, even if they occurred simultaneously, in order that the time of birth will be the ultimate identifier. At the bottom will be the signatures of the physician and witnesses and usually the hospital's own seal. A photocopy is made, notarized, and later sent to the County Recorder. The original is given to the parents.

LOCAL CITY/COUNTY ISSUED BIRTH CERTIFICATE. Upon receipt of the notarized copy from the hospital, the County Recorder enters the birth record in a record book and/or computer, for that month, if the county was fully automated. In some locales, the County Recorder will send a State issued birth certificate to the parents. In newborn adoptions, the Original birth certificate is withheld from the biological parents and sent together with an Amended version to the central office of Vital Records *at the state capital*. Years later, when an adult adoptee attempts to access his own birth certificate from *county* office of Vital Records, he is told he must apply only to the *state* Vital Records office --a dead giveaway to someone who may not know he was adopted.

STATE ISSUED BIRTH CERTIFICATE. On a monthly or quarterly basis, the County Clerk forwards a listing of all births that occurred during that period to the central office of the *State* Vital Records office at the state capital. So, for a period of some months, the newborn may not have a state issued birth certificate on file at the central state office. When the birth has been entered into the state record, the notarized photocopy of the hospital record is usually destroyed by the Country Registrar. If a newborn dies within hours or days of birth, sometimes the death certificate gets recorded *prior* to the birth certificate. This can be either a legal occurrence or a red flag indicating a baby switch or snatch – a common occurrence in the United States and Canada in the 1950s and 1960s among physicians who sold babies for black market adoption. (A "Directory of B l a c k M a r k e t Baby Brokers," by state, is included in the Addendum of this book.) Anyone born in a hospital has at least two birth certificates, each of which has legal status, while some people never get a *state* issued birth certificate and the *hospital* issued record is their only birth certificate. Midwives who routinely deliver babies will have a supply of hospital type birth certificates and will certify the document with their own stamp or embossing tool, particularly in rural southern states, with the expectation that the parents will take the midwife supplied birth certificate to the County Registrar. But often this does not happen, so federal agencies will accept the midwife's birth certificate. But if someone was to present a freshly minted looking birth certificate that does not look as old as the person described in the document, it would be suspect.

PRIVATELY ISSUED FAMILY RECORD and DELAYED BIRTH CERTIFICATE. These may be incorporated into a family record book or inside a family Bible. They were and still are quite common in rural areas of the Midwest and South. Under certain circumstances, these are not acceptable as legal proof of birth. A person can obtain a state-issued Delayed Birth Certificate years later, based on these Family Records.

CHURCH ISSUED BAPTISMAL BIRTH CERTIFICATE. In areas where the Catholic, Episcopal or other church that practices baptism is strong, a signed, sealed Baptismal Birth Record is accepted as readily as one that is state-issued, even by state and federal agencies, as legal proof of birth. The information on them is whatever the parents provide. State and baptismal birth certificates may have conflicting information, so searches should aim for a "match" of other documents, newspaper birth notices, etc.

FOREIGN BIRTH CERTIFICATE. Generally, most countries maintain records of births, deaths and marriages in a central office of civil or vital records, known by different names in different languages. Church records, in addition to or in place of civil records, can be archived going back centuries and it may be easier to utilize a genealogist or website such as Ancestry.com to search records. *The Ultimate Search Book - Worldwide Edition*, is a print edition that provides information and resources for every state and country and can be obtained either direct from the publisher, Clearfield Company, or from Amazon.com, or BN.com – or obtain FREE access by asking your local public or university library Acquisitions Librarian to order it:

AMENDED BIRTH CERTIFICATE. Prior to finalization of their adoption, adoptees have an Original birth certificate that reflects the true facts of their birth, assuming it was not a black market adoption. State laws require that, upon adoption, an Amended (legally falsified) Birth Certificate be issued which they will carry through life.

9. BIRTH INDEXES. Birth indexes are not the same as birth certificates. A birth index may cross reference mother's maiden name, father's first name, with adoptee's birth name and adoptive name. Not many birth indexes are publicly accessible any longer due to Vital Records offices learning that adoptees accessing them, as genealogists did, could discover their parents. For example, **Birth Indexes on microfilm are publicly viewable at Vital Records offices in the 5 boroughs of New York, and at your local Family History Library, but not for upstate New York.** In some states, birth indexes were purchased by genealogists and adoption searchers who sell the information.

10. INTERNATIONAL SOUNDEX REUNION REGISTRY (ISRR) is the oldest and largest free (donations only) nonprofit, voluntary registry for "next of kin" searches, whether separated by adoption or for any other reason. There are around 225,000 active registrations, at any given time. ISRR was paper based until 2003, when the volunteers began an imaging project that took five years to complete. Now all forms are digitized. ISRR was founded by the late Anthony S. Vilardi and his wife. Emma May Vilardi (now deceased), who was an adoptee and genealogist. It is now operated by its Board of Trustees – professionals who are themselves, adoption affected. Their form for submitting information is at isrr.org and by mail at: ISRR, PO Box 37119, Las Vegas, NV 89137; phone number is (775) 882-7755. To achieve a "match," Soundex first emphasizes phonetic pronunciation, spelling and filing. Most of the time the input is limited to known date and time of birth, hospital and location, and the requester's name.

11. VITAL RECORDS CROSS SEARCH. Vital Records offices cross-reference women's maiden and married names. Vital Records will search records with maiden name to find a record under subsequent married name, for a fee, plus cost of the record or copies.

12. FAMILY MEMBERS AS INFORMATION SOURCE. When searching, family members, including adoptive family members, can be the quickest, easiest source of information.

13. DEPARTMENT OF MOTOR VEHICLES (DMV) – Even a non-driver may hold a DMV- issued ID Card. Depending on the state, privacy and anti-stalking laws (such as in California) now prevent DMV from disclosing an address, but some states may give an "address verification" if you can provide the name, date of birth, and last known address. This system is routinely used by auto rental agencies. An investigator using or claiming to be a car rental agent might offer a bogus address to get the actual address. Some DMVs may, for a fee, provide a "messaging service" or forward your letter to the person at the address that DMV has on file for their driver's license or car registration, if the name is not too common and so can be readily found. In states that still permit it, DMV may have a form for requesting the current address for a person who had a driver's license in that state. Many states require a person wishing to register a car to provide a Social Security Number. States that use the person's Social Security Number for their driver's license are: DC, HI, IA, IN, ID, MA, MS, MT, NV, OK and VA. A search by a woman's maiden name often produces her subsequent married name or other name change. In states where a driver's license does not reveal the Social Security Number, it is often recorded on DMV computers when a person receives a traffic ticket, or from auto registration filings, so a numeric search can often be run if one knows the Social Security Number. THESE RECORDS BELONG TO THE STATES, NOT TO THE FEDERAL GOVERNMENT, which is why access may differ from state to state. Texas is the only state that does not notify the state of the prior license that the person has obtained a Texas driver's license–so if it appears that a driver's license has long ago expired, never been renewed, and a state does not show any transfer to another state, that person may be in Texas.

CARFAX.com, a private online company, provides a used vehicle's history for a fee, including every city and state it's been registered in, if you know the Vehicle Identification Number (VIN). If you ask a major car dealership to "Show me the CARFAX," for one of their used vehicles, they won't charge you, while small car lots will likely charge for this.

14. LAW ENFORCEMENT can run a "Driver's License Compact" in 39 states whether or not the person has any criminal record but is simply sought for legal reasons. Law Enforcement can search NCIS and DBA databases if the person had a prior criminal record. Sex Offender databases such as the national Megan's Law Registry and local versions are publicly accessible online.

15. USPS, UPS, FEDEX.

UNITED STATES POSTAL SERVICE (USPS) no longer provides address verification or disclosure service, but you can address a letter to the person's last known address and write Forwarding Order Information Requested" on the envelope, and or write "Occupant: Please forward if not at this address. If they filed a Forwarding Order within the past year, your letter will be forwarded to their current address. Or if you address your letter **"c/o** <u>Mary Jones or Occupant</u>" at her known address, the route carrier to must deliver it to whomever is at that address, but you won't know if it was received by or forwarded to Mary Jones.

UNITED PARCEL SERVICE (UPS) and FEDERAL EXPRESS (FedEx)- The "My UPS Address Book" is your own personal database for up to 2,000 shipping addresses shared with UPS.

FEDEX. A Federal Express driver can access a data bank of addresses for everyone who has ever shipped or received a package, and if addressed in error to a PO box where FedEx cannot deliver it, FedEx will automatically deliver it to a last known address while you wonder where it went.

16. SOCIAL SECURITY and THE SOCIAL SECURITY NUMBER. The Social Security Number (SSN) is a very useful piece if information. An interesting website, <u>SortByName.com</u> reveals millions of Social Security Numbers by searching with the last name, narrowed down by place or date of birth or death. It was not required that a baby's birth certificate bear a Social Security Number until the "Tax Reform Act of 1986" required parents to start putting a SSN on their tax return for children under 5. This resulted in the new practice of babies getting an SSN shortly after birth as it is now required for any "dependent" regardless of age.

The Social Security Administration no longer offers a "Locator Services" for forwarding your letter to a person whose name is not too common, along with additional identifiers and if they could be found in their database, whether dead or alive. But Social Security's Administrative Offices, which, in the past, reportedly receive only one or very few requests per month to locate a missing family member, MAY still comply with certain requests, especially if the request is accompanied by a court order or a police report of a "missing person." Like any government agency, depending on staffing, it may take awhile to hear back. A collections agency may be able to quickly track down a person's Social Security Number, which is required to access their Credit Report, and the Credit Report in turn can generate their last known and previous addresses, personal and financial information. While it is illegal for individuals to access *someone else's* Social Security or Credit information, knowing their Social Security Number can provide a wealth of information about the person's background and can more positively confirm an adoptee and parent, and where the person first received their Social Security Number.

17. THE SOCIAL SECURITY NUMBERING SYSTEM
- The first 3 digits of a Social Security Number are called the "Area Number."
- Every state is assigned a different set of these numbers, so you can tell where the person resided when they first received their Social Security Card.
- 232 was transferred from West Virginia to North Carolina.
- 574, 580, 586 were assigned to Southeast Asian Refugees (from 4/75 to11/79)
- 700-728, later discontinued, had been assigned to Railroad Retirees
- The huge <u>Find-A-Grave.com</u> website <u>SortByName.com</u> reveals millions of Social Security Numbers with dates of birth and death, by using last name to search

SOCIAL SECURITY NUMBERS ASSIGNED
by State, District of Columbia, U.S. Possessions:

416-424 Alabama	010-034 Massachusetts	408-415 Tennessee
574 Alaska	362-386 Michigan	449-467 Texas
526-527 Arizona	468-477 Minnesota	528-529 Utah
429-432 Arkansas	425-428 Mississippi	008-009 Vermont
545-573 California	486-500 Missouri	223-231 Virginia
521-524 Colorado	516-517 Montana	531-539 Washington
040-049 Connecticut	505-508 Nebraska	223-231 West Virginia
221-222 Delaware	530 Nevada	387-399 Wisconsin
577-579 District of Columbia	001-003 New Hampshire	520 Wyoming
261-267 Florida	135-158 New Jersey	
252-260 Georgia	525, 585 New Mexico	**ADDITIONS:**
575-576 Hawaii	050-134 New York	600-601 Arizona
518-519 Idaho	237-246 North Carolina	602-626 California
318-361 Illinois	501-502 North Dakota	589-595 Florida
303-317 Indiana	268-302 Ohio	587-588 Mississippi
478-485 Iowa	440-448 Oklahoma	585 New Mexico
509-515 Kansas	540-544 Oregon	232 North Carolina
400-407 Kentucky	159-211 Pennsylvania	**U.S. POSSESSIONS:**
433-439 Louisiana	035-039 Rhode Island	586 American Samoa, Guam
004-007 Maine	247-251 South Carolina	580-584 Puerto Rico
212-220 Maryland	503-504 South Dakota	580 Virgin Islands

18. THE SOCIAL SECURITY DEATH INDEX lists every deceased, non-military person who worked under or collected Social Security, and also Korean War and Vietnam War dead by name. It is useful for verifying whether the person you seek may be deceased and where the person last resided, which may lead you to search for living relatives in that area. The Death Index may be searched by joining Ancestry.com or at Reunions.com or via Mormon Family History Centers and public libraries. There are several genealogy websites that have versions of the Social Security Death Index which can reveal the SSN Number by searching it with a name (if not too common) and date of birth.

19. CREDIT REPORTS. The largest private databases of personal information are run by Credit Bureaus. The 3 largest national Credit Bureaus are Experian (Experian.com), Trans Union (TransUnion.com) and Equifax (Equifax.com). You are entitled to one FREE copy of your own Credit Reports once a year (or also if you've been denied credit) via the government's website at annualcreditreport.com, authorized by federal law for the purpose, and also directly from each of the 3 national Credit Bureaus online or by mail, and also by authorizing other companies to do so. A Credit Report may contain a wealth of information about a person, including their current and previous addresses, current and past names, date of birth, employment, credit history including types of loans, credit accounts with credit limits and balances, public records of collections, foreclosures, bankruptcy, lawsuits, wage attachments, liens and judgments, and your FICO Score (originally "Fair Isaac Corporation," founded in 1956), which is calculated by the 3 national Credit Bureaus.

14

These databases used to be "off limits" to a private investigator but the federal government now allows your information to become available to an investigator. Identifiers are needed, to access a Credit Report include the Social Security Number, Name, Date of Birth, Address and Employment. Persons who you authorize to do so include, but are not limited to: Auto Dealerships and Retailers when applying for credit, Employers, Insurance Companies you authorize for underwriting insurance, Landlords and Real Estate Rental Agents when applying to rent property. Collection Agencies and Attorneys do not need your authorization but do need authorization from the person who has a judgment against you for money you owe. Subscriber Services such as Merlin, Choice Point, Copperstone and others run credit reports for companies for a fee. A common ruse of a searcher using a business name is to claim to be doing "a Background Check" by phone, but KNOW THE LAW and don't misrepresent. For instance, California's law governing background checks (CA Civil Code §1785 et seq.) is a bit different from the federal Fair Credit Reporting Act (FCRA),

20. INVESTIGATIVE CONSUMER REPORTS. Innovis.com and CoreLogic.com track and issue reports not typically found in Credit Reports, and some credit reporting agencies and investigation companies compile what is known as "investigative consumer reports." Such reports are defined under the Fair Credit Reporting Act (FCRA) as: a consumer report or portion thereof in which information on a consumer's character, general reputation, personal characteristics, or mode of living is obtained through personal interviews with neighbors, friends, or associates. An investigative consumer report is normally used in limited circumstances including employment background checks, insurance, and rental housing decisions. An investigative consumer report does not contain information about your credit record that is obtained directly from a creditor or from you.

21. ADOPTEE and PARENT SEARCHES. **It is not illegal for an adoptee to search for his/her family, nor for a parent to seek his/her adult child.** (See Chapter 2: "WITH OR WITHOUT A NAME" for steps to shortcut one's search.) Finding out adoption information and/or finding an unknown adoptee or parent can be attempted *either passively (such as posting to a registry) or actively (by utilizing search strategies).* There are usually at least two adoption files - one held by the agency or attorney, and one held by the court. Varying degrees of information can be obtained from these files by adoptees and their biological parents. It is most important to know in what state the adoption was *finalized* – since that state, *which may be different from the state of birth*, is the state that holds the records. The quickest approach for an adoptee who doesn't know, would be to simply ask his/her adopters to see the Petition to Adopt which, in older adoptions, may even contain the names of their biological parents. The Final Decree of Adoption, which every adopter is provided by the court, and any other documents may be in their safe deposit box or elsewhere.

Lacking any documents, adopters who have little or no pre-adoption information can at least share the name and location of the public (Social Services) agency branch, or private (nonprofit) agency, or attorney *who handled the adoption, and in what court, in what state and county the adoption was finalized (which is often the county in which the adopters resided at the time),* and any verbal information provided by the agency or attorney at the time. Depending on how the fact of the adoption has been handled in the adoptive family, an adoptee may prefer not to ask their adopters for this information, but still has a normal need to know. Hence, *The Ultimate Search Book*.

15

Chapter 2 contains the chart, "ADOPTION DISCLOSURE LAWS AT A GLANCE" since it is important to know what degree of disclosure might be possible in the state, from "non-identifying information" to full disclosure and contact assistance. The chapter includes "QUESTIONS FOR ADOPTEES AND PARENTS TO ASK AGENCY AND COURT." Even in the few states where adult adoptees are permitted a copy of their original birth certificates, learning how to locate unknown family members, and how to approach them when found, can seem overwhelming... and so this book goes beyond explaining "how to" search by sharing the pros and cons of search options and contact approaches under various scenarios from others' experiences and where to find support.

22. MEDICAL RECORDS. You have a right to access Medical Records in which you are named, but conditions for access is determined by State law. In California, for instance, under the Health and Safety Code Section 123110, a patient may obtain his medical records on request, in person or by mail, by signing a Release of Records. Check your state's law by Googling or use FindLaw.com. A form may be provided by a doctor's office or hospital, but, generally, a brief letter captioned "Authorization and Release of Records," identifying the record(s) by date or approximate date and type is also sufficient. It is not required that you state a reason for the request; it is your right. You may designate that the records be sent to another doctor or other person in your behalf. A hospital's or doctor's medical record of a birth that includes the mother's record of the delivery can provide an adoptee, or a searcher in behalf of an adoptee, with the identifying information needed to find his/her biological parents. However, if you indicate you are adopted, doors will close. It's not lying or law-breaking to omit such information.

23. LIFE OR DEATH SEARCH. Over the years, Judges rarely opened a closed adoption record to an adoptee, even in a medical emergency such as to find a donor match for an organ transplant. Or, if they do open the file and locate the biological parent, and the parent refuses contact, the Court will not inform the adoptee of the parent's identity nor identities of other biological relatives. A volunteer service, only to adoptees, called "Terminal Illness Emergency Search (TIES)," may be available to quickly locate biological parent(s) – see Kinsolving's website at reunion.adoption.com. International Soundex Reunion Registry (ISRR.com) (Tip# 20) also has a "Medical Alert" service.

24. CHECKING CREDENTIALS OF DOCTORS AND HOSPITALS.
PHYSICIANS. To check physician credentials, Google the Medical Board for the state needed, and find their link for checking a physician's license. Type in the doctor's name and county where he practices. The results, (for example from the California Medical Board website), may include: If a physician has been disciplined or formally accused of wrongdoing by the Board; if a physician's practice has been temporarily restricted or suspended pursuant to a court order; if a physician has been disciplined by a medical board of another state or federal government agency, or a physician has been convicted of a felony reported to the Board after January 3, 1991; if a physician has been convicted of a misdemeanor after January 1, 2007 that results in a disciplinary action or an accusation being filed by the Board, and the accusation is not subsequently withdrawn or dismissed; if a physician has been issued a citation for a minor violation of the law by the Board within the last five

years. This is not considered disciplinary action; if a physician has been issued a public letter of reprimand at time of licensure (not considered disciplinary action); any hospital disciplinary actions

that resulted in the termination or revocation of the physician's privileges to provide health care services at a health care facility for a medical disciplinary cause or reason reported to the Board after January 1, 1995 (hospital disciplinary actions are not removed unless the privileges are subsequently restored); malpractice judgments and arbitration awards reported to the Board; malpractice settlements over $30,000 that meet the following criteria: Four or more in a 10-year period if the physician practices in a high-risk specialty (obstetrics, orthopedic surgery, plastic surgery and neurological surgery); 3 or more in a 10-year period if the physician practices in a low-risk specialty (all other specialties).

Information that is confidential and NOT public and would NOT appear on a record if applicable to the physician, under California law): Complaints made to the Medical Board of California; Investigations conducted by the Medical Board of California; Misdemeanor convictions that occurred after January 1, 2007 and did not result in an accusation or disciplinary action being filed by the Board; Some medical malpractice information, e.g., pending or dismissed cases. This information may be available at the local county courthouse in the "Civil Index." California Superior Court contact information.

HOSPITALS. To look up a specific hospital for licensing and accreditation, facilities, finances, patient services, the American Hospital Directory at ahd.com/freesearch.php is a free online service.

PSYCHOLOGISTS, THERAPISTS, SOCIAL WORKERS. These are may be grouped under the category of Behavioral Sciences or other separate state website for looking up the status of a license, any negative background, and for complaints, etc.

25. DONOR OFFSPRING/PARENT SEARCHES and DNA TESTING. Donor conceived persons, like adopted people, express a normal desire to know about the unknown person whose genes they carry. Increasingly their anonymous donors have been wanting to know about the children they helped conceive. Americans For Open Records (AmFOR) provided the only totally free registry for Donor Offspring, Donor Parents, and Siblings, a *passive* method that relies on both parties registering, *now discontinued due to maintenance cost,* and instead provides easy to follow information in this book, for an *active search,* including:
• Tips for Offspring & Donors (on Searching, Posting, Connecting)
• How to Locate Using Name Search
• Affordable DNA Testing (Links)
• More Online Resources(Links)

26. FIRST NAME/AGE ONLY SEARCHES, AND CHILD UNDER 18. Generally, High School yearbooks on Classmates.com or at public libraries, for the year and city where the person may have graduated high school have been good resources for finding someone with only a first name, age, including adoptees and parents. By successfully matching up limited identifiers or non-identifying information with physical characteristics in yearbook photos, you then have a name (or possibly more than one "possible") to check out. For children under 18, see Chapter 2 : "WITH OR WITHOUT A NAME" and Chapter 3: "MISSING AND RUNAWAY CHILDREN" - Usually searchers will not undertake a search for a child under age 18, especially in divorce situations, as custody orders or restraining orders may hinder the non-custodial parent's personal proximity

or contact. So a searching parent concerned for their child's welfare but prevented from knowing the child's whereabouts, especially in adoption situations, might narrow down the public and private schools the child may be attending in a likely area. If you're uncertain about the grade level for the known age of a child, ask the school board office, without mentioning that you're searching for your child. If you must state a reason, it is sufficient to indicate that you are looking at homes for sale and would like to be near a school that accommodates a child of the specific age.

27. MISSING ADULTS. Always notify Law Enforcement when you have reason to believe an adult is missing. And have available a photo of the person with their detailed description, and a list that includes their close friends and relatives, employer, and places they frequent on a regular basis such as clubs gyms, social groups etc. (which can turn up someone who witnessed the person having been last seen at a specific location). Before expanding your search, phone those most likely to know of the person's whereabouts – to verify that the person hasn't simply lost track of time while visiting with that person. If these preliminary actions don't turn up the missing person, see Chapter 4: MISSING ADULTS, for steps you can take to locate a missing adult.

28. CITY, COUNTY, STATE and COURTHOUSE PUBLIC RECORDS can be viewed free, even borrowed free in some locales depending whether they are paper records or on computer, or faxed or mailed for a fee. Public records include "vital records" -- birth, death, marriage and divorce records (except birth records of adoptees or others that may be sealed by a court); property and property tax records; business licenses; civil case information; traffic citations and certain criminal case information, etc., but cases involving children in family court, juvenile court, and probate court are confidential.

29. BETTER BUSINESS BUREAUS. BBBs serve businesses through BBB accreditation and serve consumers who may file complaints about a business's practices and determine the trustworthiness of the business via BBB's local websites

30. IF YOU ARE DENIED ACCESS TO RECORDS. Most records of the Court and Vital Records offices are intended to be "public records" but clerks may refuse access to some to which you are ordinarily permitted access. You are also entitled to Police Reports in which you are named or that are related to a matter for which you are charged with a crime. Witness statements may have witness names blocked (blackened) for the witness' protection. Rape victims' reports may be confidential. If you are denied access or a copy, you will need to phone the local Bar Association or State Attorney's office, or provide the clerk or his/her supervisor with your written Freedom of Information Act (FOIA) request and ask (with a recorder on) "Under what grounds am I being denied access?" and name the record and person refusing on the recording, in case you need to file a formal complaint. (See Search Tip #20 in this chapter, "Freedom of Information Act and the Privacy Act.")

31. CORRECTING A RECORD. If a record has significant errors (other than harmless typos), you are entitled to have the record corrected. Whether by brief letter identifying the record and error, or by court order depends on the kind of record. During litigation, a record related to the litigation in

need of correction needs to be presented or argued at a hearing since the judge may need to decide its accuracy (for instance if it's in regard to testimony or evidence) according to judge's *discretion*. After a case is closed, generally the record cannot be changed except by creating a subsequent record on appeal. Correction of a pre-adoption birth certificate is often denied because, technically, once it is sealed, it no longer "exists" in law.

32. STATE and FEDERAL PRISONER LOCATOR WEBSITES. If the person you seek has or may have a criminal record and is *presently* incarcerated by a **STATE** Department of Corrections (DOC), a (Free) nationwide Inmate Locator is at https://www.thefreeinmatelocator.com/ - (FIRST, select the state from the alphabetical list of states at the Left of the page to bring up the Inmate Locator site for that state). For some states, however, you may need to request the location of an inmate by phoning or writing to the State Department of Corrections. To locate a **FEDERAL** prisoner, use the (Free) Federal Inmate Locator at https://www.bop.gov/mobile/find_inmate/byname.jsp Some State DOC websites also identify the county jail where the person may be held, or may indicate that the person is currently released on probation. If so, the probation office for the locale can tell you the name and contact information for the person's probation officer who, in turn, may be able to tell you where to contact the person or may agree to pass a message to the person when they comply with periodically reporting to the probation office. A l s o t r y M u g s h o t s . c o m . Genealogy databases may include old prison records in U.S. and other countries.

33. DNA TESTING, MATCHING. DNA tests have long been used to prove paternity and family relationships for inheritance. But now DNA can also be utilized to find one's biological relatives via DNA registries. Tests and registration is available from a number of sources in their database, but, like Adoption Reunion Registries, DNA cannot be "matched" unless a relative's DNA results from a biological relative is on the same "Registry," so it is recommended that the "top 3" services be utilized and watch for "sales" – For instance, 23&Me now advertises periodic sale pricing, especially on holidays such as Christmas, such as $60 instead of $99. They are:

- 23&me - (Autosomal) – 23&me.com
  and Upload DNA Test Results (just from 23&Me) to GedMatch.com
- o Ancestry.com (Autosomal and Y-Chromosome)- AncestryDNA.com
- Family Tree DNA (Autosomal) FamilyTreeDNA.com

You can opt to receive notification of any "matches" but they may be for distant cousins or a first cousin match can most easily start your genealogical search for their immediate relatives and narrow it down to "possibles" such as sisters – one of who could be your mother – and this book provides further help in locating her.

You can also create a page on Facebook with your DNA results for matching to possible siblings, others.

The Federal Innocence Protection Act that entitles a wrongfully convicted person to Post-Conviction DNA testing by a designated lab, upon court approval.

19

34. VOTER REGISTRATION. Voter registrations are public records in County Clerks' offices. You can write for them but it will take forever to hear back. Especially in cities understaffed or cutting services to the public to save costs. In many area, these records are available online. If not, a trip to the County Clerk's office may be your best bet.

35. FEDERAL RESOURCES include "The Federal Parent Locator," used to access Internal Revenue Service (IRS) tax records (IRS records are not "public" records, though tax accountants routinely and legally tap into certain IRS databases); Social Security records (previously detailed in this chapter); military locator services (see Search Tip #36 for all branches of military); National Archives Office of Disclosure, and Immigration and Naturalization Services (INS) records. NCIC - THE NATIONAL CRIMINAL IDENTIFICATION CENTER (N C I C) database is not accessible by the public. DO NOT TRY TO OBTAIN INFORMATION FROM A FEDERAL EMPLOYEE THAT IS NOT NORMALLY OBTAINABLE WITH A FREEDOM OF INFORMATION ACT REQUEST (See Search Tip #39 for more on FOIA requests).

36. THE NATIONAL CENSUS can be used to conduct a search by age and are a source of genealogical information, but the Census Bureau does not provide these data, nor is the Census Bureau is not able to locate missing persons, or provide *recent* information on individuals. The Census Bureau provides an "age search" service to the public by searching confidential records from the Federal population censuses of 1910 to 2010 and will issue an official transcript of the results for a congressionally mandated fee. The Census Bureau Home page is at https://www.census.gov/#. NOTE: Information can be released *only to the named person, his/her heirs, or legal representatives.* Individuals can use these transcripts, which may contain information on a person's age, sex, race, State or Country of birth, and relationship to the householder, as evidence to qualify for Social Security and other retirement benefits, for Passport Applications, to prove relationship in settling estates, in genealogy research, etc., or other situations where a birth or other certificate may be needed but is not available. Contact the National Processing Center at (812) 218-3046 (FAX is (812) 218-3371. There is a fee required for a search of one Census for one person only. Personal checks and money orders accepted. No credit cards. Years Searched: 1910 through 2010. Census records with individual names are not on computer. They are on microfilm, arranged according to the address at the time of the census. Most agencies require the earliest Census after the date of birth. A completed BC-600 Application form [PDF] is required for Search of Census Records, signed by the person for whom the search is to be conducted. This person may authorize the results to be sent to another person/agency by also completing Item 3 of the Application. Information regarding a child who has not yet reached the legal age of 18 may be obtained by written request of either parent or guardian. A guardian must provide a copy of the court order naming them as such. Information regarding mentally incompetent persons may be obtained upon the written request of the legal representative, supported by a copy of the court order naming such legal representation. With regard to deceased persons, an Application must be signed by (1) a blood relative in the immediate family (parent, child, brother, sister, grandparent), (2) the surviving wife or husband, (3) the administrator or executor of the estate, or (4) a beneficiary by will or insurance. In all cases involving deceased persons, a copy of the Death Certificate MUST be provided and the relationship to the deceased MUST be stated on the application. Legal representatives MUST also furnish a copy of the court order naming such legal representatives, and beneficiaries MUST furnish legal evidence of such beneficiary evidence. An official Census transcript will list the person's name, relationship to household head, age at the time of the census, and state of birth. Citizenship will be provided if the person was foreign born. Single items of data (such as occupation for Black Lung cases) can be provided upon request.

If a person is <u>not</u> found, a form will be sent to inform you. Additional data on the same person, called the "Full Schedule" is the complete one-line entry of personal data recorded for that individual ONLY. This will be furnished in addition to the regular transcript. Additional charge (in 2014 was $10, but ask) for each full schedule. Not available for 1970, 1980, 1990 and 2000. State of birth and citizenship is only available in Census records from 1910 to 1950. Normal processing time is 3 to 4 weeks, and processed on a first in, first out basis. Passport and other priority cases can be processed in a week or less, for an additional fee to receive results within 3 days; the application will need to be sent by Next-Day Air via USPS, FEDEX, or private carrier with pre-paid Express return envelope enclosed. Applications can be faxed to you.

37. TELEPHONE RECORDS, UNLISTED PHONE NUMBERS, ADDRESSES. Public Directory listings by Name and City/State at <u>WhitePages.com</u> (which is still free) may include the person's listed phone number and sometimes an otherwise unlisted/unpublished phone number as result of the person having divulged their phone number on an unsecured website, or to a company that shares or sells mailing lists with such information to advertisers. <u>People Search.com,</u> <u>Intellius.com</u> and <u>Spokeo.com</u> will sell same-name listings that include address and phone number without guarantee that they are current. <u>MyLife.com</u> is known to have inaccurate information but can provide names of relatives, last known addresses, etc. Public libraries maintain databases compiled from nationwide mailing lists which are sold and re-sold (hence those annoying unsolicited sales calls, even to your unlisted number). Cell phone companies are one source of such lists as subscribers often forget or are unaware that they must opt out or specify that their phone number is not to be listed or published.

Directory Assistance Operators may share an address, especially if you state that you need to be sure you have the right party at the right address before dialing the number to avoid being charged for a wrong number. If the operator refuses, or will only share the street name but not the house number, simply dial back--you'll get a different operator who may be more willing or able.

Licensed private investigators, like Law Enforcement, may be able to obtain phone records and non-published phone numbers from telephone service representatives, using only name and zip code. The general public may be told that telephone operators and service representatives do not have access to these numbers, but if, for instance, you owe money, you can bet a collections agency will have your phone number in an instant.

Amateur searchers can possibly elicit such information using ruses, but if they make a false representation especially in a phone call that crosses state lines, be aware that is then a federal crime that has resulted in arrest by the FBI and imprisonment of not only the searcher impersonating an official to get information across state lines, but also the person who headed the organization in which the searcher was employed with headquarters in yet a different state. (See Disclaimer at the front of this book, and more about harmless ruses versus prosecutable offenses in the final chapter: "STARTING YOUR OWN SEARCH BUSINESS.")

38. OCCUPATIONAL, RECREATIONAL LICENSES and REGISTRATIONS.

LABOR UNIONS will not cooperate with Law Enforcement but private searchers have been successful in eliciting information for locating people via their Labor Unions by claiming they need to get in touch with the person due to a family emergency. CAUTION: If someone offers to leave a message instead, avoid doing so, since you will then be sharing your phone number without knowing theirs and you don't want to start off on the wrong foot by having to explain that you made up a story to get their phone number. So, instead, explain to the person at the Labor union that it's a delicate matter that may upset the other person to hear it from a stranger and is best told by a supportive relative/personal friend but you've lost the number. If this goes against your personal ethics, then simply ask to "verify the phone number which may have been changed." This implies you had the number to begin with, and any number you suggest will be wrong and hopefully the person will provide the correct one. Some agencies may also provide proof of an Occupational License but with identifying information blackened out. Such a record may still be helpful to verify an occupation, etc.

HUNTING AND FISHING LICENSES are public records which disclose last reported address etc.

39. FREEDOM OF INFORMATION ACT and THE PRIVACY ACT:

You can obtain a copy of The Federal Freedom of Information Act (FOIA), and THE PRIVACY ACT online (see foia.gov and Wikipedia for The Privacy Act of 1974.), or from your public library, or from your local Congressman's office without charge. Although the two laws were enacted for different purposes, and pertain only to records held by FEDERAL agencies in a "system of records" retrieved by name or personal identifier, there is some similarity in their provisions. There may be a difference in fees, time limits and exemptions from access.

STATE FOIA LAWS in every state pertain only to state-held records. The FOIA laws by state, are available online at the State Freedom of Information Coalition (NFOIC) website at nfoic.org/state-freedom-of-information-laws by clicking on the abbreviation for the name of the state. Some state FOIA laws contain multiple exemptions of records that cannot be accessed, even under the State FOIA.

The FEDERAL FOIA gives "any person" the right to access, while THE PRIVACY ACT gives only the person named in the record the right of access.

Sample letters for obtaining records using the FOIA can be found online also.

If you request records about YOURSELF under both Federal and State FOIA laws, federal agencies may withhold records from ONLY to the extent that they are exempt under BOTH federal and state FOIA. FOIA requests require fees. But if you want any information about yourself without fees, just cite The Privacy Act. If in doubt as to which law will satisfy your needs, cite both. In any case, you need to "reasonably describe" the specific record(s) you seek to avoid delay from not sufficiently describing the record.

To obtain records about OTHER PEOPLE, the FOIA contains an important provision about personal privacy: "Exemption 6" protects you from others who may seek information about you and it may also block you if you seek information about others. Exemption 6 also permits an agency to withhold information about individuals if disclosing it would be "clearly unwarranted invasion of personal privacy," but Exemption 6 cannot be used by an agency to withhold information about you.

22

Therefore, searchers sometimes request information in the name of the person the information is about. To be covered by Exemption 6, (1) The information requested must be about an "identifiable" individual; (2) an invasion of that individual's personal privacy if disclosed to others; (3) clearly unwarranted" to disclose.

ADOPTEES AND THE FOIA. Yet the FOIA exempts adoptees' own birth records by vaguely wording the law while at the same time the law recognizes the adoptee's basic human right to know his own identity and origins. No one has yet successfully challenged adoption secrecy laws under the FOIA and Privacy Act because the United States Supreme Court simply refuses to hear such cases, as tried by ALMA Society v. Mellon, and Yesterday's Children v Kennedy in the 1970s. What made Carangelo v. Connecticut in 1990 "different" was that the U.S. Supreme Court deferred to the state legislature, despite that it presented an important challenge to the *federal* Constitutionality of "government protected child stealing under color of state adoption secrecy laws." For legal case cites, read "*Carangelo v. Connecticut*" (available on Amazon).

40. HIRING A LICENSE PRIVATE INVESTIGATOR {PI). PI's usually do not have the resources or desire to complete adoptee/birthparent searches. If you are considering hiring a licensed Private Investigator to conduct an adoption search, ask the PI for his/her resume, references, license number, whether he/she is bonded, *and, for names of people for whom they successfully completed adoption searches*. The best detectives have ample experience, and the best indicator of that is word of mouth, because reputations are hard won in this business. A bond larger than the minimum may be available for a broad investigation that could cover several states or even a foreign country. Interview him or her for at least 20 minutes to discuss your needs and how they would be met. Check the state licensing division to be sure the PI's record is clean, and require a signed agreement defining fees and the specific service(s) to be provided within a time frame, with periodic reporting if likely to take a considerable amount of time, or stating that you require that the PI document what they did and observed. Times have changed for PIs. Instead of snapping incriminating photos to support claims in divorce cases, modern "private eyes" earn bigger fees from corporate spying, security and personnel matters. They are often more effective than police in tracking down runaway or missing children because they can focus on leads for a single client, whereas a Missing Persons Bureau may have 30 cases at a time. If a PI *cannot* produce a hard lead *within 3 days*, s/he may be incompetent or may be stalling to run up the bill.

41. ADOPTION SEARCHERS. (See also "Chapter 2: "With or Without a Name.) Amateur searchers, as well as agencies who charge search fees may or may not have a "No find, no fee" policy so always ask for specific terms and whether they have "tools of the trade" such as innovative technical devices and computer programs, databases, and /or a network of paid or volunteer searchers to tap. In a TNT Network TV series, *"APB with Troy Dunn*," Dunn, aka "The Locator," unites separated loved ones using technology and a phone app to solve the case within the minutes between TV commercials. However, behind the scenes, in the real world, solving "impossible searches" usually requires tipsters and cash that someone has to be able to afford… or a dedicated "Search Angel" who most often is a birthmother or an adoptee who now works tediously without compensation to help other adoptees and parents of closed solve their adoption puzzle. (See 'RESOURCES and WEBSITES" section)

In the 1980s, before computers were commonplace in every office and household, and through the 1990s, AMERICANS FOR OPEN RECORDS, which maintains a page on Facebook at https://www.facebook.com/AmFOR.net/) reunited 20,000 families by developing a network of

individuals throughout the United States, Canada, the United Kingdom and Australia, and also learned techniques applicable in other countries, to assist adoptees and parents in overcoming the roadblocks that separated them. And it was all done by mail and phone. We often published their stories and provided media with their "live" reunions to acquaint the general public with the idea that "nothing bad" happens when adoptions are opened up. A m F O R n o longer conducts searches, but this book can expedite completion of one's search.

42. SEARCH WORLDWIDE. The worldwide search network consists of thousands of professional, semi-professional and lay-researchers including adoption searchers (most of whom are, themselves, adoptees and parents) and also genealogists. Some searchers will work only on a one-to-one basis while others work only through group membership and support.

Local search and support groups and individuals tend to specialize in their local area. National search and support groups usually require a membership fee and may hold meetings. Individuals and groups that offer search assistance may also belong to an umbrella organization such as Concerned United Birthparents cubirthparents.org the American Adoption Congress (AmericanAdptionCongress.org), Bastard Nation (Bastards.org), for a unified presence in media, and for lobbying, fund raising, book sales, and/or annual national conference lectures, workshops, demonstrations. Americans For Open Record (AmFOR) is no longer active but continues to publish adoption-themed books available in both Kindle and Paperback at Amazon.com/dp/B001KCH348/ - - *or ask your local library to order them*.

43. REAL ESTATE LISTINGS. Type a street address with city and state in the search field at Zillow.com and it will bring up the real estate listing for the home whether or not it is currently for sale and provide information about the type and age of the home, the area it's in, when it originally and last sold and for what price, its suggested current value, exterior and interior photos, etc. Search Google.com and it may bring up a 360-degree aerial view and street view that can be manipulated to enable a virtual drive-through in the neighborhood and beyond, unless a gated/restricted community.

44. MILITARY PERSONNEL AND RECORDS. Americans For Open Records (AmFOR) created an "ADOPTEES' WAR MEMORIAL" page on Facebook, consisting of many scrollable news articles about individual adoptees, each captioned with their names and photos, of those who served in the U.S. Military and who sacrificed their lives for their country – yet were not permitted to know who their biological parents are, due to state sealed records laws. The page is at https://www.facebook.com/Adoptees-WAR-Memorial-1706323576282550/ The Department of Veterans Affairs has a Nationwide Grave Locator site at gravelocator.va.gov/ for locating deceased military personnel. Or, to find active, former/retired, or deceased military personnel or records, each branch of the military has its own department(s) to assist according to the status of the person (see below for address and phone number –

45.   Check online in case of change of address or phone.). When writing to any branch of service, your request should include at least the following information, or, if many of he items are unknown, at least the first 5 items: (1) Full name under which the military service was performed; (2) Social Security Number; (3) Dates of Service; (4) Date and Place of Birth; (5) Residence of service member at time of entry into the service; (6) Branch of service; (7) Reserve status, Branch and dates; (8) Last known address; (9) Grade or Rank; (10) Name and Address of Service Person's Parents; (11) Organizations with approximate Dates Assigned (the most significant ones).

But when little information is known, one technique for preventing return of the inquiry for "insufficient information" (whether online or by mail) is to approximate or make up some of the unknown information and see what comes back, perhaps auto-corrected. A service person may obtain all the information in his/her own record.   The person's next-of-kin, if the veteran is deceased, and federal offices, for official purposes, are authorized to receive certain types of information. Other requesters need permission of the service person. Fees are determined at the time the records are released, but you should always inquire as to how fees are calculated – for instance, a per-page copy fee with minimum fee for under "x" number of pages.

If you are adopted but know the name of one or both of your biological parent(s) and that they were military personnel at one time, in order to be considered "next of kin" for purpose of obtaining information or records. Omit any mention of being adopted.

AIR FORCE. For all reserve members not on extended duty and all retired reservists in a non-pay status: Air Reserve Personnel Center, 3800 York Street, Denver, CO 80205-9998. For all Active Duty personnel, all personnel on a temporary disability retired list (TDRL), general officers in a retired (pay) status: USAF Military Personnel Center, Military Personnel Records Div., Randolph AFB, TX 78148-9997; (210) 656-2660 (will only confirm in writing).

ARMY. Officers separated before July 1, 1917, enlisted personnel separated before November 1, 1912:   National Archives and Records Service, National Archives Building, Washington, DC 20408. All retired personnel, all Reserve personnel (includes retired Reservists): Commander, U.S. Army Reserve Personnel Center, 9700 Page Blvd., St. Louis, MO 63132-5200. All officers on active duty: Commander, U.S. Army Military Personnel Center, Management and Support Div, Officer Records Branch, 200 Stovall St, Alexandria, VA 22332-0400.   Enlisted personnel on active duty: Commander, U.S. Army Enlisted Records and Evaluation Center, Fort Benjamin Harrison, IN 46240-5301; (703) 325-3732 (will only confirm in writing).

ARMY NATIONAL GUARD. All members not on active duty in the U.S. Army, personnel discharged from the National Guard (excludes records of periods and active duty for training in the U.S. Army): The Adjutant General (of the appropriate state, DC, or Commonwealth of Puerto Rico). Records for periods of active duty or training for the U.S. Army for periods ending after December 31,1959: Headquarters, Department of the Army, Office of the Adjutant General, U.S. Army Reserve Components Personnel and Administration Center, 9700 Page Blvd., St. Louis, MO 63132.

COAST GUARD: Enlisted personnel separated less than 6 months, Officer personnel separated less than 3 months, all active Coast Guard members of the Reserves, Officer personnel separated before January 1, 1929: Commandant, U.S. Coast Guard, U.S. Coast Guard, Washington, DC 20221-0001; (203) 227-2229 (will confirm some by phone).

MARINE CORPS. Officer personnel on active duty or in Reserves, enlisted personnel on active duty or in organized active Reserves, all personnel completely separated less than 4 months: Commandant of the Marine Corps, Headquarters, U.S. Marine Corps, Washington, DC 20380-0001; (703) 784-3942 (will confirm by phone).

NAVY. Officers on active duty, or separated less than one year, all Officers with rank of Admiral, enlisted personnel on active duty, those separated with less than 4 months, active and inactive Reservists with 18 or more months remaining in first term: Chief of Naval Personnel, Department of the Navy, Washington, DC 20360-00011 (901) 874-3388 +2 (will confirm by phone).

ALL BRANCHES. If your request does not pertain to any of the above categories, address an inquiry to: ATT: (appropriate branch of service) Records, 9700 Page Blvd., St. Louis, MO 63132

VETERANS REUNIONS INFORMATION: VETS, PO Box 901, Columbia, MO 65205; (573) 474-4444. Also" REUNIONS, VFW Magazine, 406 W. 34th St, Ste. 523, Kansas City, MO 64111.

WWII VET FATHERS information is available as result of WAR BABES 1988 lawsuit. Contact the Dept. of Defense, Pentagon, Washington, DC (They will not provide the street address.

CIVIL WAR SOLDIERS and SAILORS. To locate either a Union or Confederate Civil War Soldier or Sailor by name, there is an online database. A Soldiers and Sailors Index or Database at nps.gov/civilwar/index.htm, sponsored by the National Parks Service, is a free service – most other websites for finding Civil War soldiers may offer free registration but then charge for access to their databases and/or records. For descendants of Confederate Soldiers, the following provides links, by state, to resources – jrw3.tripod.com/do.htm.

MILITARY, WAR and LINEAGE SOCIETIES - CYNDI'S LIST has several pages of Links to these websites – cyndislist.com/societites/lineage/military

45. PASSPORT SERVICES AS AN INFORMATION SOURCE. If you're an adoptee who is denied your original birth certificate, applying for a passport can generate the Passport Office's request for your original birth certificate. The "Amended" (falsified) version issued to adoptees may be considered a "Delayed" record, or could be withheld as "fraudulent" or "suspicious," or at best in need of followup, if, depending on date of your adoption, the date of issue is months or years later than date of birth. Passport Services needs the original to verify citizenship. WHAT TO DO: Request to the court to provide YOU with an Order ordering Vital Records (the one at the state capital) to release your original birth certificate to YOU for purpose of obtaining a passport – by attaching proof of a copy of your Application for a Passport and the response from Passport Services. This has worked for some when the clerks release the birth certificate to the adoptee instead of to Passport Services. If your immigrant ancestors returned home to visit family or to bring relatives to America, they may have had a U.S. Passport. To obtain passports prior to 1906, write to: Diplomatic Records Branch of the National Archives, Washington, DC 20406. For Passport applications after 1906, write to: Passport Office, U.S. Department of States, 1425 "K" Street, Washington, DC 20406.

46. MEDIA ACCESS TO INFORMATION AND RECORDS. A source of non-legal advice for accessing information and records is your local newspaper and TV station's investigative, since they need to know the law and how to legally obtain information, with or without a court order.

If you have a good news story or human interest story to share, they may be willing to obtain information or records to back up your story. A reporter won't reveal his sources but may be able access sealed files by court order for a "major" story or point you to files that you can access.

47. MEDIA SUPPORTED SEARCHES. Local media attention to a search for a missing person can garner community support with people joining the search. National media attention to an adoption mystery can produce leads or even solve the case. In #48, below, a court denied my request to open my son's record based on Medical Good Cause, but publicity about my issue drew the attention of a searcher who quickly found my son for a price.

48. GOOD CAUSE. In any state, regardless of any provisions for disclosure, an adoptee has the right to request that the court open his/her adoption file "for Good Cause." Because state law does not specifically address *what* constitutes "Good Cause," the matter is entirely at the discretion of judges, who usually deny the request, citing "privacy" of the "birth" mother, despite that sealing of records was never requested but was imposed by state law. (If you know your "birth" mother is *deceased,* see "Adoption Search Tips # 9," next chapter.) In the 1980s. this author requested that Judge Glen Knierim of Connecticut's Probate Court open her son's adoption file "for Good Cause (Medical)." Connecticut law at the time allowed adoptees but not the adoptees' biological parents to communicate important new medical information. In my case, it was my newly discovered inheritable heart defect and my inheritable allergies to the prescription drugs that commonly treat it. Judge Knierim was quoted by a journalist as saying the reason he denied the request was *"because the law doesn't compel me to do so."* This is why anyone contemplating a "Good Cause" action should consult and be represented by an attorney and why adoptee-birthparent groups bypass the courts to contact each other directly. A controlling case that can be cited in a letter petition to the court seeking to one's original birth certificate when the birthparents are deceased, to support the fact that "privacy ends with death," is: Davin v. U.S. Department of Justice, 60F.3d1043 (3rd Circuit 1995)

49. 'WORD OF MOUTH.' People can be excellent sources of information when the information they are willing to share can be verified. It's important to regard verbal information as a "lead," rather than an absolute fact. Neighbors can be a good source of information depending on your approach, for instance, if you're thinking of buying a home and was wondering whether it is a quiet street, whether the residents are in your age group, etc. An adoptee's unknown parent's name, spelled out by a sympathetic social worker at risk of her job in a medically urgent situation, is probably reliable but still requires verification and followup to locate. Consider the source and verify!

50. ONE SEARCH ENDS, ANOTHER MAY BEGIN. While most searches may end when the person sought is located, after an adoptee who finds their biological mother, the next question usually asked is "Who is my father?" (See Adoption Search Tip#10, "Finding Dad," in the next chapter.)

2019 Adoption Disclosure Laws At A Glance
(Always check for recent law changes)

A=Adoptee; P=Parent; AD=Adopter; S=Birth Sibling; CI=Confidential Intermediary; COO=Court Order Only; OBC=Original Birth Certificate

State	Non-ID	Search Procedures	Records Access
Alabama	A,AD	Passive Registry=P; CI	OBC-A
Alaska	A,AD	Passive Registry=P	OBC-A, at age 18
Arizona	A,AD,P	CI=A,AD	COO
Arkansas	A,AD,P	Passive Registry=A, S, P; CI=A, P ; Counseling req.	COO
California	A,AD,P,S	Waiver System=A, P,S	COO
Colorado	A,AD	CI= A, P, S; Passive Registry= A,P	COO/veto post-"99
Connecticut	A,AD,P	CI· Adult access to OBC finaled on/after 10/1/83	COO OBC-
Delaware	A,AD,P	Active Registry=A, AD ; P veto	OBC-A, age 21
District of Columbia	No Provisions	No Provisions	COO
Florida	A.AD	Passive Registry=A, AD P; CI=A, P	COO
Georgia	A,AD	Active Registry=A, S; Passive Registry=P	COO
Hawaii	A,AD,P	Active Registry=pre- '91, A; post '91=veto	COO
Idaho	No provisions	Passive Registry=A,S,P	COO
Illinois	A,AD	Passive Registry=A, S, P; CI	COO
Indiana	A,AD,P	CI=A, P; Passive Registry=A ,P (S=restricted)	COO
Iowa	A,AD	Passive Registry=A, P	COO
Kansas	A,AD	Active Registry=OPEN to A age 18	OBC-A, at age 18
Kentucky	A,AD	CI=A, Passive Registry=P, S,AD with consent of P	COO
Louisiana	A,AD	Passive Registry=A pre-'81, A, P with counseling	COO
Maine	A,AD	Passive Registry= A, AD, P	OBC-A pre-6/1/47
Maryland	A,AD,P	Passive Registry= A, P;CI	COO
Massachusetts	A,AD,P	Waiver System=A, P	COO
Michigan	A,AD,P,S	Waiver/Registry/CI=A, P,S	COO
Minnesota	A,AD,P	Active Registry/Waiver=A, P,AD=post"82/P-veto	COO
Mississippi	A,AD	CI=A, P; Registry=post-'94	COO
Missouri	A,AD	CI, Registry† Adult access to OBC- A,B,S; Lineal;	OBC-born pre-1941
Montana	A,AD	Passive Registry=A, P; CI= AD, P veto	OBC=pre '67; COO
Nebraska	A,AD	Waiver/Active Registry=A	OBC-A age 25;P veto
Nevada	AD	Passive Registry, A,P	COO
New Hampshire	A, P	Waiver/Agency-CI=A, P	OBC=A age 18
New Jersey	A	No Provisions	COO
New Mexico	A,AD, P	Passive Registry=A, P	COO
New York	A,P	Active Registry=A,P; CI; Public BirthIndex 5 boroughs	COO
North Carolina	A,AD,P	No Provisions	COO
North Dakota	A,AD	Waiver/Active Registry= A,AD,P,S	COO
Ohio	No Provisions	Passive Registry=A, P, S	OBC-pre1964
Oklahoma	A,AD,.P	Passive Registry=A, P; CI	COO
Oregon	A,AD,P	CI=A,AD,P	OBC=A,age21
Pennsylvania	A,AD CI=A;	Passive Registry=P; Medical Registry	OBC=A, w/P waiver
Rhode Island	A,AD.P	Passive.Registry=A, P	COO
South Carolina	A,AD, P	Passive Registry=A, P	COO
South Dakota	A,AD	Passive Registry=A, P	COO
Tennessee	A,AD	Active Registry=A, P	OPEN to A; veto
Texas	A.AD	Passive Registry=A, P	COO
Utah	A,AD,P	Passive Registry=A, P	COO
Vermont	A, AD,P	Waiver at Central Registry=A, P, pre-'86 with consent; veto	COO
Virginia	A.AD	CI=A, P	OBC-A at age 18
Washington	A,AD,P	Passive Registry=A, P ; CI	COO
West Virginia	A,AD	Passive Registry, A,P	COO
Wisconsin	A,AD	Active Registry=A; Passive Registry=P	OBC=A w/ P consent
Wyoming	A.AD	CI; Registry=AD, P	COO

Medical and health information in an adoption file is generally that which was available at time of placement. Only 8 states (AL, IL, KS, MD, MN, MN, MS, WY) allow Adopters to request that the state adoption registry contact "Birth" Parents when additional health information is medically necessary.   **2019: 11 states (AL,AK,CT,DE,KS,MO,NE,NH,OR,TN,VA)** provide certain adoptees **Original Birth Record on request;** CT,OH,ME,MT,PA,WI access depends on date adoption finalized or Parent Consent; in all other states and District of Columbia, American Samoa and Puerto Rico, a Court Order is still required and/or require mutual consents/waivers or Confidential Intermediaries. In the 5 boroughs of New York, anyone can view Birth Indexes which cross-reference birth and adoptive names, but not elsewhere in New York. All states (and American Samoa) now have provisions in statutes that allow access to Non-Identifying information by an Adult Adoptee (at age 18 or older) upon written request, or by an Adopter or Guardian of an Adoptee who is a minor. Non-identifying information depends on availability or social worker discretion, and may include date and place of Adoptee's birth, ages of "Birth" Parents at time of placement, and general physical descriptions, race, ethnicity, religion, family medical history, "Birth" Parents' educational level and occupations at time of adoption, reasons for placement, existence of other children born to each "Birth" Parent. Approximately 15 states allow biological adult Siblings of the Adoptee to seek and access Non-identifying information; 36 states allow adult biological Siblings to seek and release Identifying information upon mutual consent.

2021 - DEGREE OF ADOPTEE ACCESS
TO ORIGINAL BIRTH CERTIFICATE, BY STATE

STATE	STATUS	STATE	STATUS
Alabama	Unrestricted Access	Montana	Partial with Restrictions
Alaska	Unrestricted Access	Nebraska	Partial with Restrictions
Arizona	Sealed	Nevada	Sealed
Arkansas	Access with Restrictions	New Hampshire	Unrestricted Access
California	Sealed	New Jersey	Access with Restrictions
Colorado	Unrestricted Access	New Mexico	Sealed
Connecticut	Partial Access	New York	Unrestricted Access
Delaware	Access with Restrictions	North Carolina	Sealed
District of Columbia (D.C.)	Sealed	North Dakota	Sealed
Florida	Sealed	Ohio	Access with Restrictions
Georgia	Sealed	Oklahoma	Partial with Restrictions
Hawaii	Unrestricted Access (adoptions in HI) + Sealed (births in HI with adoptions outside of HI)	Oregon	Unrestricted Access
Idaho	Sealed	Pennsylvania	Access with Restrictions
Illinois	Access with Restrictions	Rhode Island	Unrestricted Access
Indiana	Access with Restrictions	South Carolina	Partial with Restrictions
Iowa	Sealed	South Dakota	Sealed
Kansas	Unrestricted Access	Tennessee	Access with Restrictions
Kentucky	Sealed	Texas	Sealed
Louisiana	Sealed	Utah	Sealed
Maine	Unrestricted Access	Vermont	Partial with Restrictions
Maryland	Partial with Restrictions	Virginia	Sealed
Massachusetts	Partial Access	Washington	Access with Restrictions
Michigan	Partial with Restrictions	West Virginia	Sealed
Minnesota	Partial with Restrictions	Wisconsin	Access with Restrictions
Mississippi	Sealed	Wyoming	Sealed
Missouri	Access with Restrictions		

Chapter 2:
WITH OR WITHOUT A NAME
Families Separated by Adoption or Divorce

- privacy - (the state of not being seen by others by one's own choice)
- confidentiality - (imposed in a discretionary manner, avoiding accountability)
- secrecy - (imposed concealment, enabling coverup, avoiding accountability)

Americans For Open Records (AmFOR) has, for years, successfully completed "No Name Searches" which are searches without a known name to start, usually due to closed adoption, or due to divorce that may entail a stepparent adoption by the custodial parent and where the absent parent may have changed their name from re-marriage. This chapter reveals techniques that adoptees and parents can utilize for obtaining the unknown name, and for adoptees and children of divorce searching for biological family members, and for parents searching for their children.

STEP 1 - WHICH STATE? There are usually two adoption files – one held by the public Social Services (or private adoption agency or attorney), and one filed in the court since adoptions are *finalized* by a court. An adoptee, or a parent who has voluntarily relinquished or otherwise lost a child to adoption, first needs to know in what state the adoption was *finalized*, which is often the adopter's state of residence, so the court of jurisdiction may be the court may also be in the county where the adopter resides. But also, a child may have been adopted out of state via an attorney or private nonprofit adoption agency. If you don't know, and Social Services finds no record, it may be that it was a private adoption. In the past, many agencies failed to try to collect sufficient information on a child's biological family and pre-adoption past, or provided as little "summarized" information as possible, even *untrue* information, while others provided a great deal of factual information, or even actual records may be provided on request, though they may have been r e d a c t e d (names blackened out). As the times, politics, laws and attitudes changed, so did their methods and extent of collection and disclosure of adoption information by some agencies.

STEP 2 - WHAT'S THE LAW?
When you know which state finalized the adoption, you can find out what the current state law is "for post-adoption disclosure" in that state (which could be a different state from the state in which the adoptee was born). State laws now mandate provision of at least "Non-Identifying" background information to the adult adoptee. Some states also provide Non-ID to the parent or adopter. On the previous pages, you will 2 charts listing the states, alphabetically - one indicating what, if any, disclosure and to whom, and how disclosed (as of 2019), and one chart indicating Adoptees degree of access to their original birth certificate (as of 2021).

NON-IDENTIFYING INFORMATION. All states now mandate by law the provision of "Non-Identifying" information to an adult adoptee. Not all provide Non-Identifying information to biological parents or adopters. Approximately 15 states allow biological adult siblings of the adoptee to seek and access Non-Identifying information.

Non-identifying information can provide useful clues for discovering identities and locating the other person, depending on what information was collected at the time of the adoption, but also may inform the adoptee of his/her family's previously unknown nationality, parents' ages at time of the birth and/or adoption, the adoptee's age when adopted, the parents' race, religion, education level, employment, pre-existing siblings, circumstances, etc. Parents can discover the adopters' ages at time of the adoption, nationality, race, religion, education level, employment, pre-existing children by birth or adoption, etc. Every state now mandates, by law, that public and private adoption agencies and attorneys must provide adult adoptees and their biological parents with each other's non-identifying background information upon written request, usually with proof of identity and age such as a driver's license. If you're the adoptee, your letter should list at the top your adoptive parents' full names (since your adoption file is filed by their names); your date and place of birth, the date and state your adoption was finalized, if known; and any other known related names, dates, places, and your Waiver of Confidentiality. Ask ALL of the questions on the list below, even if you believe you already know some of the answers.

If you're the parent who lost a child to adoption, your letter should begin with your child's date and place of birth, agency or attorney that facilitated the adoption and in what county and state, your full name at time of the relinquishment, any other known related names, dates, places, your current contact information and Waiver of Confidentiality. Ask ALL of the questions listed below, even if you believe you already know some of the answers.

WAIVER OF CONFIDENTIALITY. If both the adoptee and parent have provided their "Waiver of Confidentiality" to the adoption agency, attorney and/or court, identifying information and contact may be facilitated in states that permit it post-adoption. Such a Waiver may not need to be on a specific form for the purpose. There may be a letter from the adoptee or parent, placed in the adoption file, stating that the adoptee or parent waives their confidentiality in the event the other party seeks information or contact in the future. It may or may not require notarization but it's always a good idea to do so. If, when your Waiver form or letter is placed in the adoption file, the other party's Waiver is already in the file, you may be informed of any further steps required to enable contact with the other party, depending on state law and agency policy and procedure.

POST-ADOPTION REUNION REGISTRIES. Due to a proliferation of private online and offline adoptee-parent reunion registries, including over 400 listed by Adoption.com at reunuin-registries.adoption.com/ most adoption search and support organizations now advise their members to register primarily on the (free) private nonprofit INTERNATIONAL SOUNDEX REUNION REGISTRY at isrr.com (See Tip #7 for details) to take the control away from agencies. But it cannot be searched online, so you must remember to update your contact information if you have a change of address or phone because ISRR will need this to inform both parties if there is a "match." Large, free, online registries include Cyndi's List at CyndisList.com and The Seeker at theseeker.com.

A California registry, "Find My Family Registry" findmyfamily.org/California had over 11,000 registrants and could be searched online.

In states that offer a State Adoption Reunion Registry via the agency that facilitated the adoption, it is more often a matter of providing such a Waiver to the file, so may not have instantaneous results, although some agencies now have on online registry. In past years, there was a proliferation of private adoptee-parent-sibling reunion registries which provide registration online or by mail. Online registries can be searched by either party. Some are totally free while others require a one-time or annual membership fee, and an abundance of registries may lessen the chance of a random "match" if the other party is not clairvoyant to know on which the first party may have, by chance, registered.

BIRTH ANNOUNCEMENTS in newspaper archives may automatically been published in a newspaper if a notation stating "Do Not Publish" by hospital staff was not evident at the time to advise that the newborn is to be adopted. When searching for a birth notice, request a range of up to 4 weeks AFTER date of birth. Whether the newspaper maintains archives online, or whether you can order copies of actual new clips direct from the newspaper office's "morgue" or "library" for a copy fee, or from public libraries, they may reveal the parents' names to a searching adoptee.

MARRIAGE RECORDS, DIVORCE RECORDS, VOTER REGISTRATIONS, PROPERTY OWNERSHIP AND TAX RECORDS. In states where marriage and divorce records are public records, a vital records office may be able to cross reference a mother's known maiden or married name at time of the adoptee's birth with any subsequent name change via divorce and later marriage records. When you have a name, voter registrations, property ownership and Tax assessments at Tax Assessor's office are always public records. There is also usually a Real Estate Index at the County Courthouse, a courthouse Litigation Index, court dockets (of even adoption hearings and dockets are public records, not sealed) while there is restricted access to the court Petition to Adopt and Final Decree of Adoption.

Other publicly accessible records include Church Baptismal Records (see Search Tip #5); Mormon Family History Center Library records of births and genealogies worldwide; White Pages directories, especially WhitePages.com; Yellow Pages and other business directories; Criss-Cross directories, and High School Yearbooks (see Search Tip# 3).

QUESTIONS FOR ADOPTEES TO ASK AGENCY AND COURT:

1. What was the reason for my relinquishment?
2. What were the ages of my parents?
3. Where were my parents born, and where did they reside at the time of my adoption? Were they from same area where I was born?
4. Name of hospital where I was born?
5. What are the nationalities of my parents?
6. Were my grandparents living?
7. Educational background of my parents and grandparents?
8. Occupations and social history of parents and grandparents?
9. Any siblings?
10. Were parents married? Divorced? Previous marriages?
11. Religion of parents?
12. Was I in a foster home? How long? Who were my foster parents?
13. How long between relinquishment & placement?
14. Was my mother in a maternity home? Did she see & hold me? Was she counseled before/after delivery or signing?
15. Color of parents' hair? Eyes? Their height? Weight?
16. Did my parents have brothers, sisters? Ages?
17. Mother's first name and initial?
18. Did she name me? What name?
19. Were my parents active in school activities? What kind?
20. How much did I weigh at birth?
21. Has my mother or any birth family member EVER contacted the agency? Any letters, photos or mementos in my adoption file? Is there any Waiver of Confidentiality in my adoption file?
22. Name of social worker handling my placement?
23. Date adoption was finalized? What court(s) initiating, finalizing?
24. Please provide me a copy of the court proceedings and final decree.
25. Please provide me with all medical information on my birth family.
26. Please place my Waiver of Confidentiality in the agency file.
27. Please contact my parents and inform them my updated Waiver of Confidentiality has been provided to the file.

QUESTIONS FOR PARENTS TO ASK AGENCY AND COURT:

1. Regarding the adopter(s):

a. what were their ages?	h. deaths in family?
b. where were they born?	i. medical histories, diseases?
c. what are their nationalities? religion?	j. did they own their own home?
d. any siblings of adoptive parents?	k. professions, occupations, education?
e. length of marriage at time of adoption?	l. where residing at time of adoption?
f. any previous marriages or divorces?	m. where do they now reside?
g. other children by birth or adoption?	n. reason given for adopting?

2. Regarding the child, please provide physical description when last seen by agency, court or attorney.

3. Was child in foster care? How long? Names of foster parents?

4. Date adoption was finalized? What court?

5. Please provide a copy of the relinquishment I signed and the original birth certificate issued to me.

6. What is the name of the social worker who handled the placement?

7. Has adoptee or adopter(s) contacted agency since adoption?

8. What was and is my child's physical and emotional health?

9. Were the adoptive parents advised to tell child of adoption?

10. What information on me was given to adoptive parents?

11. Please place my Waiver of Confidentiality in the file.

12. What agency/court/attorney will transmit my request for contact to the adoptee or adopter(s)?

Adoptees and their biological families confront an adversarial adoption system designed to thwart their efforts to locate each other. It has been reported by some that even when both parties have registered on state-sponsored mutual consent voluntary registries, state agencies fail to "match" and inform the parties that each has registered and have consented to be contacted. The state usually does not publicize their registries or law and policy changes nor solicit a missing Waiver of Confidentiality in behalf of the other party who has submitted their Waiver and desires information and/or contact. And when they do inquire, they may have to pay hefty fees and wait months for a response. Los Angeles County Social Services, for example, often took a year to respond. When individuals complete searches on their own, some discover that each was registered with the state for a year or more, or that each had informed the agency and/or court of urgency for medical or other reasons, or that the other party has died. Still, state registries should not be overlooked as reunions have resulted for those who cannot or do not wish to actively search, or who wish to utilize every means available.

MORE ADOPTION SEARCH TIPS (which may also apply to stepparent adoptions):

1. READ CHAPTER 1: SEARCH BASICS.

2. DETERMINE THE STATE in which your adoption was *finalized* because that's where the court (and probably the agency) holds your adoption file(s).

3. DETERMINE THAT STATE'S LAW on disclosure of adoption information and records, particularly access to original birth certificate (see Charts, pages 28-29, but also check for changes).

4. LOCATE YOUR ADOPTION FILE(S). Ask your adopters which agency and court facilitated your adoption. If your adopters did not save records, you can inquire at *the central office of Social Services at the state's capital city,* whether yours was a public Social Services agency adoption and which branch. If no record, chances are it was a private agency or attorney, which Social Services would not have record of. Since the Court that *finalized* the adoption is usually in the county where the adopter resided at the time of placement, it would not be too hard to find the Court and agency that has your adoption file(s) by looking up the Court and adoption agencies in that county. If no luck, then try adoption *attorneys* in that county. By law, in most states, you're entitled to at least "Non-identifying information" which can provide clues for gaining identities.

5. REQUEST NON-IDENTIFYING INFORMATION from both the Court of jurisdiction *and* the agency that holds your adoption file, by asking ALL of the Questions listed in this chapter.

6. PROVIDE YOUR WAIVER OF CONFIDENTIALITY and your request for identifying information to both the agency and court at the same time you request your Non-Identifying Information. Request the original Petition To Adopt and Final Decree of Adoption from the Court.

7. BROWSE THE COURT DOCKETS for the dates you were relinquished for adoption and also when the adoption was finalized (generally finalized automatically, without necessity for hearing, but there will still be a Docket notation) *one year from date of Relinquishment of Parental Rights and placement in your adoptive home.* Court dockets are *publicly viewable records* in Probate, Circuit, and Family Courts or similar named courts, not sealed. Even though your biological parents most likely were not in court, their names may appear on the earlier Docket while your adopter's name appears on the later Docket. They can be cross-referenced by same Case Number, so if you find the Final Decree case number by the date, you can check *one year prior* for the Relinquishment and Petition to Adopt by using the same Case Number.

8. REQUEST THE PETITION & FINAL DECREE OF ADOPTION. Years ago, Court Clerks were instructed to "block" (redact) names on these documents with an indelible black ink marker before providing the document to the adult adoptee. Unless the blackened information has also been photocopied after blackened, first try photocopying the BACK side of the document *on a very dark setting* to see if typewritten impressions appear, or try penciling the back of the document where the names would be, thereby revealing the names (just backwards). Try removing the black marker ink with a dab of alcohol or alcohol based hairspray, last, since this will wet the document.

9. DECEASED PARENT OR ADOPTEE. If denied records on the grounds that the person is deceased, cite the following: <u>Davin v. U.S. Department of Justice</u>, 60F.3d1043 (3rd Circuit 1995): Persons who are deceased have no privacy interest in non-disclosure of their identities."

10. FINDING DAD - REQUEST YOUR HOSPITAL RECORD OF BIRTH. Obtaining the hospital record of your birth may fill the gap left by records that do not identify your father, or may address the question as to whether the person who was named as your "legal father" due to marriage was likely *not* your biological father. This is only feasible if you know your mother's name when you were born. Request "the complete record for both mother and newborn, including: Admissions Record (which may indicate who paid (perhaps your father or other relative), doctor's and nurse's notes, newborn photo and/or footprint, delivery room record and discharge record." Do NOT indicate you are "adopted," even if you know your bio parents' names, or the Medical Records will likely deny you access.

11. APPLY FOR A PASSPORT. Read details on page 26 - One technique some adoptees have used successfully for obtaining a copy of their original birth certificate otherwise denied them, is to apply for a passport because a (true) birth certificate will be required. Request that the court provide you with an "Order for Vital Records (at the State capital) to Release Original Birth Certificate," and attach a copy of your Passport Application, and the Response, as proof that it is needed for that purpose.

12. YOUR FOSTER CARE RECORDS ARE *NOT* SEALED RECORDS. Most adopted children are placed in foster care at least temporarily while awaiting completion of a home study for placement in their adoptive home. Many adoptees were in more than one foster home and for a longer period before adoption. One of the questions (#12) to ask when requesting non-identifying adoption information was whether you were in foster care and the names of your foster parents. Foster Care records are confidential but not "sealed" records, so it is common for former foster kids to re-visit foster parents who treated them well, so you may be able to obtain your foster care records by written request with identification (a copy of your driver's license), and thereby discover your biological parents' names as well. Valid reasons would be (1) you wish to see and thank your foster family; (2) you wish to locate your siblings (whether or not you actually have sibs); (3) for any medical or health information which your doctor informed you would be helpful in diagnosing you

13. CHECK NON-PROFITS THAT MAY HAVE LOCATOR SERVICES. Mothers were formerly residents of Salvation Army Maternity Homes and Hospitals, and adoptees who were placed by agencies after birth at Salvation Army facilities have their own *registries* and search support groups online, by state. Searching Salvation Army mothers and adoptees at The Seeker – theseeker.com

14. BLACK MARKET ADOPTEES. Try "Black Market Adoptees' Registry" at webring.org, Baby Brokers by state (in Addendum of this book), and
DOBSEARCH.com for date-of-birth search in cases where the name may be changed.

15. THE CONFIDENTIAL INTERMEDIARY SYSTEM. The states have been amending laws by requiring use of a Confidential Intermediary (CI) for the purpose of opening the adoption file and locating the biological parent at the request of the adult adoptee and to communicate the adoptee's desire for information and/or contact. A CI can be appointed by a court or can be an adoption agency social worker, depending on state law. CIs charge a non-refundable fee and are not permitted to divulge identifying information unless both parties agree. So there is a risk that the adoptee will gain nothing by paying a CI except the knowledge that either the CI did not locate the mother within the maximum hours the CI devotes to the task, assuming that an effort was made, or that the mother refused contact and any information including updated family medical information, thereby also preventing a search for the adoptee's biological father (if, for instance, the mother will not provide that information). Because what, how and for whom a CI performs this duty is entirely at the CI's discretion, AmFOR and this author encourages adoptees and parents to instead do their own searches, if possible, and to make their own direct contacts, rather than have a go-between attempt to deliver the messages and ask questions that both of you have had to wait years to communicate. But sometimes this is not feasible. In one case, AmFOR persuaded a Court appointed CI in Washington State to waive her fee for a Washington adoptee's biological grandmother who resided in California, because her daughter, the adoptee's biological mother, had died, and we provided proof to the court of the grandmother's low income (it never hurts to ask). The CI was able to locate the adoptee who then resided in neither Washington nor California, and he was glad to be found as he had no idea how to begin a search and could not afford a CI either. The CI charged only for the cost of long distance calls. In another case, an adult adoptee incarcerated in Michigan was first denied even non-identifying information by Sister Joanne Ales, who headed Catholic Social Services of Macomb County. AmFOR donated the $60 fee by check, but Ales, who expressed disdain for all prisoners, returned AmFOR's check and required $250 from the prisoner to instead act as Confidential Intermediary, an obvious conflict of interest. Catholic Social Services in a different county in the same state of Michigan provided another incarcerated adoptee with his non-identifying information that disclosed his father's first name. For a current list of Confidential Intermediaries, contact the Court, or Social Services, or the private agency involved, or Google "Confidential Intermediary" and the state name.

16. INCARCERATED ADOPTEES OR PARENTS are subject to the same state laws and rights for disclosure as other adoptees/parents, regardless of crime for which convicted, or bias of the person holding the adoption file. Typically, a prisoner's Central File does not indicate adoptive status. Google the "Prisoner Locator" website for the state needed to search using inmate's name .

17. NATIVE AMERICAN ADOPTEE SEARCH RESOURCES. The 1978 Indian Child Welfare Act gives special preference in adoptions of Native American Children to the child's immediate relatives and tribe. Yet there have been highly publicized court cases (such as the Dusten and Veronica Brown case, aka the "Baby Veronica" case), where a Native American child was adopted across state lines by a non-Indian couple over the objections of the Native American parent who wanted to raise her. Adult adoptees may find the Bureau of Indian Affairs helpful in identifying the tribe to which they belong. (The Mexican equivalent is The National Indian Institute.) However, the Bureau and the tribes must still abide by state law. So "how to" search information is still essential for Native Americans searching for family members separated by adoption.

18. INNOVATIVE, BIZARRE SEARCH METHODS OF ADOPTEES AND PARENTS.
Birth indexes that cross-reference birth and adoptive names used to be easily accessed by card-carrying genealogists. Adoptees and parents have also reported resorting to more desperate actions, not advocated and which this book is designed to make unnecessary per their true stories, as follows: (1) A nationwide "search underground" has existed for many years whereby mothers have placed $2500 cash or some other amount in a Federal Express envelope addressed to open records activist, Jane Servadio, in Milford, Connecticut, who then puts them in touch with the anonymous underground searcher who provides the adoptee's identity and more; (2) An adoptee succeeded in cracking open his adopters' safe to find adoption papers; (3) a close friend of an adoptee went to the courthouse and requested to see the adoption file as if the adopter; when the Clerk asked for ID, the friend explained her name had been changed due to divorce and remarriage; the Clerk never blinked and the friend then provided the adoptee with her mother's name; (4) quickly accessing a Birth Index Book of the old printed type at courthouses when the Clerk is out on break; (5) peaking at one's adoption file that a social worker (sometimes intentionally) leaves on her desk while she's out of the room; (6) one of 8 siblings adopted separately and who learned their biological mother had died, determined where her grave was located and left a note in a bottle at the grave site. The reunited siblings erected a new tombstone for their mother inscribed "Mother's love brought us together –8 Little Orphans."

19. FAMILIES SEPARATED BY DIVORCE. There are two kinds of child custody - legal custody and physical custody. A non-custodial parent, in law, is one with whom the child does not live but may have varying degrees of contact with their child or none at all for any number of reasons. Children separated by divorce also experience inequities of archaic state "confidentiality" laws. While in cases of abuse, restraining orders and forced separation may be necessary, in most divorce situations, the parents' inability to get along results in the child losing contact with one of his parents. If the custodial parent remarries, and the new spouse adopts the child, the same secrecy of records is imposed on a child in stepparent adoptions. Some of these children may know who their missing parent is. but others may not if the separation occurred when they were very young. If it's the mother who has remarried, the child is usually given the stepfather's name. If it's the biological father who has remarried, the adopting stepmother may be listed as the mother *at time of the stepchild's birth on an "amended" birth certificate* and the child's original birth certificate is sealed (withheld) by law, as in any adoption and the same adoption disclosure laws apply. Links for Child Custody Laws, by state, are at singleparents.about.com/od/legalissues/a/custody.laws.htm. Resources on FACEBOOK for non-custodial parents include websites dealing with "parental alienation," "corrupt family courts," "CPS Watch" at Facebook.com/CPSWatch, or the National Hotline at 1-800-CPS-WATCH. Local helplines for child support problems are found at About.com which has links to every state's CUSTODY LAWS, as well as web pages with links for Fathers' Rights, Mothers Rights and "no fee legal help" for Single Parents.

Chapter 3:
MISSING and RUNAWAY CHILDREN

Since 1967, the federal government has operated a computerized National Crime Information Center (NCIC), originally used to catch criminals and recover missing property. In 1975 the Feds allowed local police to include skimpy information about missing persons. In 1982, Senator Hawkins proposed expanding the service to include listings by blood type, dental records, scars, and other information that would also help identify missing children. Since 1884, out of 945,000 annual entries into the FBI's NCIC database on missing persons, about 80% or 765,000 have been missing children.

The United Nations Special Rapporteur on Abducted Children determined, in the United Nations "Rights of the Child" Report that "the United States is the largest market for stolen children in the world, and California is the largest market for stolen children in the U.S." A child can sell for $80,000 or more for adoption, sex or pornography.

IF YOUR CHILD IS MISSING:

STEP 1 - LAW ENFORCEMENT, AMBER ALERT - America's Missing Broadcast Emergency Response. Immediately call your LOCAL law enforcement agency for an "AMBER ALERT" WITHIN 30 MINUTES from when you first perceived your child is missing. IT IS A MYTH THAT YOU MUST WAIT 24 HOURS BEFORE CONTACTING POLICE. Prompt notification to your local Amber Alert system has proven to rescue children.

If your child is missing from home, search through: closets, piles of laundry, in and under beds, inside large appliances, vehicles – including trunks, anywhere else that a child may crawl or hide. If your child cannot be found while shopping in a mall or large store, notify the store manager or security office. Then immediately call your local law enforcement agency. Many stores have a "Code Adam Plan" of action in place. Law Enforcement and child rescue teams urge parents to assemble an ID packet on each child each year with a color photo and fingerprints, and to teach a child to cause a commotion if a stranger grabs them, to have a child play and travel in groups, never leave a child alone in a car, and pick up a child from school and activities on time.

WHEN YOU CALL LAW ENFORCEMENT: Provide law enforcement with your child's name, date of birth, height, weight and descriptions of any other unique identifiers such as eyeglasses and braces. Tell them when you noticed your child was missing and what clothing he or she was wearing. Request law enforcement authorities immediately to enter your child's name and identifying information into the FBI's National Crime Information Center Missing Person File.

If your child is displaced during a disaster, immediately call your local law enforcement. Then fill out an Unaccompanied Minors Registry form. This tool lets NCMEC assist emergency management personnel on the ground in their efforts to reunite families during disasters such as hurricanes, tornadoes or terrorist attacks.

Authorities in Washington state believe now-deceased serial killer, Joseph Kondro, abducted, raped, and murdered as many as 70 young girls -- most still missing, their bodies hidden in the forests of the Pacific Northwest. But the Kondro would only confess to two of them in a plea bargain that saved him from Washington's Death Penalty. *In "KONDRO - The 'Uncle Joe' Killer,"* by Lori Carangelo, the author explains how a whole community kept a deadly secret that enabled a killer to continue his evil deeds for many years, undetected, and attempt to elicit clues (such as his favorite places for fishing, places he worked or visited at the time a girl went missing) via his correspondence over time, in hope of finding those still missing, in order to help bring closure for the victims' families.

STEP 2 – THE NATIONAL CENTER FOR MISSING AND EXPLOITED CHILDREN (NCMEC), at 1-800-THE-LOST (1-800-843-5678). When you call NCMEC, a Call Center specialist will record information about your child. A NCMEC case management team will next work directly with your family and the law enforcement agency investigating your case. They will offer technical assistance tailored to your case to help ensure all available search and recovery methods are used. As appropriate NCMEC case management teams:

- Rapidly create and disseminate posters to help generate leads.
- Rapidly review, analyze and disseminate leads received on 1-800-THE-LOST (1-800-843-5678) to the investigating law enforcement agency.
- Communicate with federal agencies to provide services to assist in the location and recovery of missing children.
- Provide peer support, resources and empowerment from trained volunteers who have experienced a missing child incident in their own family.
- Provide families with access to referrals they may use to help process any emotional or counseling needs.

CHILD ABUSE. Consider whether the child may be hiding from someone in a position of trust and authority, such as a counselor or group leader, who could be secretly abusing the child, physically, emotionally or sexually. Runaways also hide from street gangs, drug dealers, parental and school authority, or due to problem relationships, pregnancy, etc.

TEEN RUNAWAYS. If a runaway is old enough to possess a driver's license, car, Social Security Number and other ID, and is likely to work at a particular job or has predictable habits, the runaway may be making a paper trail that can be followed and reveal addresses, contacts, and any aliases used. Older, more resourceful teens may become street survivors for a time, but they can fall victim to drug dealers and prostitution. Check rescue shelters in suspect areas. CHILDREN OF THE NIGHT has rescued over 100,000 children from prostitution and offers a variety of services for them to have a good future – childrenofthenight.org - 1-800-551-1300 (24-hour Hotline).. BOYSTOWN and GIRLSTOWN National Hotline counsels and informs via a variety of recorded options or via direct discussion with a counselor about problems and programs at 1-800-448-3000.

IDENTIFYING RECOVERED CHILDREN: Local police may provide free child ID cards and fingerprinting services. Know where your child's dental and medical x-rays are. There are websites offering "child safety products" such as ID cards and shoe tags and "child print ID kits." In cases where a child has been abducted as an infant and held for a long time, they may have no memory of their family. Computer enhanced age progression of a photo of the child can aid Law Enforcement and families still searching for a child who may be two or more years older. Private investigators can devote more time to current and "cold cases" of missing children and have developed inside resources.--See also National Missing and Unidentified System (NamUs) in Chapter 4, page 38.

STEP 3 - FACEBOOK AND HELPLINES. Posting a missing child's photo, description, date and time the child went missing (and from where, possible destinations if a parent abduction, etc) on Facebook with your contact info and/or your local law enforcement phone number

Chapter 4:
MISSING ADULTS

An astounding 2,300 Americans are reported missing every day, including both adults and children. But only a tiny fraction of those are stereotypical abductions or kidnappings by a stranger. The federal government counted 840,279 missing persons cases in 2001; all but about 50,000 were juveniles (classified as anyone younger than 18). The National Center for Missing Adults, (Let's Bring Them Home, LBTH.org/, based in Phoenix), consistently tracks about 48,000 "active cases," says president Kym Pasqualini, although that number has been bumped up by nearly 11,000 reports of persons missing after devastating hurricanes. And slightly more than half of the 48,000 missing—about 25,500—are men. About 4 out of 10 missing adults are White, 3 of 10 Black, and 2 of 10 Latino. Among missing adults, about one-sixth have psychiatric problems. Young men, people with drug or alcohol addictions, and elderly citizens suffering from dementia make up other significant subgroups of missing adults. While Law Enforcement is the first step in getting help to find a missing child or adult, they may need convincing that the person is, in fact, missing, or they may be working 30 cases at a time and so may not be able to produce leads *quickly*. This chapter provides self-help steps to locate missing adults. Simultaneous combination of resources is advised.

STEP 1: LAW ENFORCEMENT - If you are missing someone, call law enforcement immediately... time is of the utmost importance. With each tick of the clock when someone is missing, the odds of finding them is go down. It can sometimes be difficult to convince police that an adult has not voluntarily left and there may be a wait time before law enforcement will even take such a report or act on it. Consequently, you should provide sufficient reason to convince them that the person's absence is *highly unusual*, or that you have reason to believe they have Alzheimer's, are a danger to themselves or others, that there may be foul play (such as if the person had received threats or been harassed before they went missing), or that they disappeared without their car or wallet/purse.

STEP 2: LOCAL MEDIA - Your local TV News station(s) will inform you as to what is required before they can publicize that a person is missing. Media attention can be the quickest way to find someone, especially if the likely circumstances of the disappearance is known - such as a hiker known to have left for a hike in a specific area has not returned when expected, or someone who started on a trip, locally or at a distance, never reached their known destination or meeting at a scheduled time and can't be reached via their cell phone. Time can be critical for a missing person with a medical condition requiring daily treatment.

STEP 3: FACEBOOK and HELPLINES have been known to solve such cases by immediately alerting people to be on the lookout for the missing person, not only in the last known area seen but also by social media voluntarily networking nationwide. Local, National and International Organization and Helplines can be found by Googling key words such as "Missing Adult Organizations" or "Missing Adult Helplines"

SILVER ALERTS, for example, a ncmissingpersons.org/current-silver-alerts is a public notification system to broadcast information about missing persons – especially seniors with Alzheimer's Disease, dementia or other mental disabilities – in order to aid in their return.

THE NATIONAL MISSING AND UNIDENTIFIED PERSONS SYSTEM (NamUs) at NamUs.gov/ is a national centralized repository and resource center for missing persons and unidentified decedent records. NamUs is a free online system that can be searched by medical examiners, coroners, law enforcement officials and the general public from all over the country in hopes of resolving these cases.

The Missing Persons Database contains information about missing persons that can be entered by anyone; however before it appears as a case on NamUs, the information is verified. NamUs provides a user with a variety of resources, including the ability to print missing persons posters and receive free biometric collection and testing assistance. Other resources include links to state clearinghouses, medical examiner and coroner offices, law enforcement agencies, victim assistance groups and pertinent legislation. The Unidentified Persons Database contains information entered by medical examiners and coroners. Unidentified persons are people who have died and whose bodies have not been identified. Anyone can search this database using characteristics such as sex, race, distinct body features and even dental information. The newly added UnClaimed Persons database (UCP) contains information about deceased persons who have been identified by name, but for whom no next of kin or family member has been identified or located to claim the body for burial or other disposition. Only medical examiners and corners may enter cases in the UCP database. However, the database is searchable by the public using a missing person's name and year of birth. When a new missing persons or unidentified decedent case is entered into NamUs, the system automatically performs cross-matching comparisons between the databases, searching for matches or similarities between cases.

NamUs provides free DNA testing and other forensic services, such as anthropology and odontology assistance. NamUs Missing Persons Database and Unidentified Persons Database are now available in Spanish.

Chapter 5:
GENEALOGY EARCHES

"In about four generations or so, about half the ancestry of the American population will be bogus," according to Attorney Brice M. Clagett, (in *"Adoption Laws Threaten the Death of Genealogy,"* National Genealogy Society -NGS Newsletter) because in all states, adoptees' birth records name the adopters as parents *on day of birth* s their ancestry in public records is *bogus*.

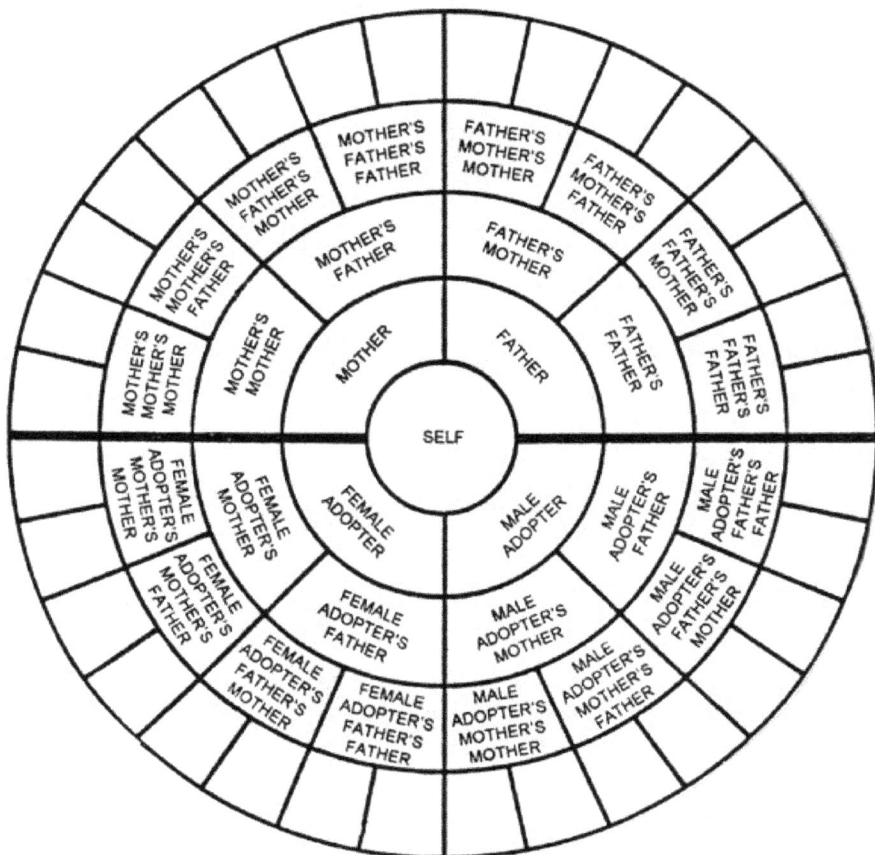

An Adoptee's "Family Wheel"

STEP 1: YOUR IMMEDIATE FAMILY. So great anyone's "natural need to know" our roots, it's not surprising that Ellis Island's Immigration Center's website had 8-million visitors in its first 8 hours of existence...and that the average person spent about $700 annually on genealogy (according to Elizabeth Bernstein, Wall Street Journal columnist in an interview on MSNBC back in 2001). The number of online researchers increase each year, as do their postings and software such as "Family Tree Maker-6th Edition." Tracing early Americans can be tricky. Few people in colonial times had three names but may be identified by their occupation without a comma: "John William Carpenter" in 1875 was probably John William - a carpenter. "John Henry Taylor" may have been John Henry - a tailor. Some wills and deeds were indexed by occupation and name. Many immigrants, or their children, "Americanized" their names, particularly movie stars. Benny Kubelski became Jack Benny. A genealogy approach can be useful for adoptees who may know the name of a blood relative, living or deceased, on one side of his biological family, which can then lead to identities on both sides of the family.

STEP 2: THE MORMON CHURCH and ANCESTRY.com - a Treasure Trove of Worldwide Genealogy Records. The Mormon Church of Jesus Christ of Latter Day Saints has amassed the largest depository of worldwide genealogical records - over 600-million names, extracted from vital records worldwide. Genealogy is an important part of the LDS faith. Their genealogy library is headquartered in Salt Lake City, Utah, with Family History Center branches everywhere. Their microfilmed and recently digitized records are mostly "more than 50 years old" but pertain to everyone - not just Mormons - and many foreign births can be researched using not only their Family History Center branches but also their website at familysearch.org. To find a Family History Center in your area for browsing microfilm records free of charge, call 1-800-346-6044 or visit the web site. At www.familysearch.org you can check ancestral files, Census records, birth and death records, and the Social Security Death Index (you don't need to know the Social Security Number if the name is not too common).

STEP 3: OTHER ONLINE RESOURCES:

INTERNET- **Ancestry.com** is the leading commercial web site for genealogy. Ancestry.com has over one million paid subscribers, and although they charge a fee to access their census records, passenger lists and other databases, the monthly fee starts at about $10 and also gives you access to Rootsweb.com, Genweb.com and other sites rich in genealogical content.

CLASSMATES.COM now enables viewers, without charge, to browse or upload for free entire high school yearbooks that are donated, and to upload your photo and profile. A membership fee allows you to contact other members.

FACEBOOK.COM still offers totally free registration to create your own Facebook page, to access pages by other individuals and groups. (for example "All Carangelos" is for anyone named Carangelo in Italy, the U.S. and worldwide), for social contacts as well as for tracking down living and ancestral relatives, further enabling anyone to grow their family tree with a click of a mouse. Family trees an be a simple keepsake album of photos of immediate relatives with their names and dates and places of birth and death for your children and grandchildren, but can also preserve the stories handed down through your family which make it interesting.

STEP 4: CASTLE GARDEN and ELLIS ISLAND.   Castle Garden in New York's Battery served as America's first immigration station from 1830-1891 before Ellis Island opened in 1892. The 10 million immigrants who passed through Castle Garden's doors were mostly from Northern and Western Europe. Castle Garden's immigration records can be searched via its "one step" passenger lists by the person's name or ship name stevemorse.org/ellis/cg.html/ Find your ancestor by name on ship's manifest in one step, free at ellisisland.org/search/passSearch.asp - the ship's manifest is printable, if you right click at the top of the frame and select Print Preview, adjust for size and select Landscape instead of Portrait, though it may not capture the image edge to edge.

STEP 5: NATIONAL AND STATE ARCHIVES (NARA) FOR GENEALOGICAL RESEARCH. The National Archives and its many branches can be great resources for the genealogical researcher. There are also Archives branches by region. If you are unable to visit a National or Regional Archives in person, you can hire someone to do so, or simply write requesting the location of the information you seek and cost per page for copies. Types of records that can be browsed, rented or purchased from National Archives is explained at archives.gov/research/order/.

- NARA has genealogical workshops, and presentations at 7th and Pennsylvania Ave., NW, Washington, DC 20408, (202) 501-5400

- The Suitland Reference Branch of the National Archives (4205 Suitland Road, Suitland, Maryland, for personal visits; Washington, DC 20409 mailing address, (301) 763-7410) has more Federal records than any branch in the U.S. They include: Bureau of Land Management (1760-1890) land entry files and homesteads, War Relocation Authority (1940-1945) Japanese Americans Interned during WWII, Dept. Of State passports (1906-1925), U.S. District Court for D.C. (1800-1960), Patent and Trademark Office (1836-1919),

- The branch at College Park, Maryland, has no genealogical records, but has Nixon Presidential Materials, Center for Electronic Records, Cartographic Reference, Motion Picture, Sound and Video, and Still Picture collections.

- For records relating to military personnel in the National Archives, it's the National Records Center, 9700 Page Avenue, St. Louis, Missouri 63132 (Army: 314-538-4261; Navy, Coast Guard, Marines: 314-538-4141)

- To research American Indians and Alaska Natives (as early as 1774) (including individual ancestry), military records, and to order copies of records, these National Archives records can be accessed online at archives.gov/research/native-americans/index.html/ - or write to: The National Archives and Records Administration, 8601 Adelphi Road, College Park, MD 20740-6001. Their Customer Service line is happy to answer questions and to direct you to the right branch of the Archives for specific tribes at 1-866-272-6272

- RECORDS AVAILABLE TO SEARCH. Not only the National Archives, but also many major libraries throughout the United States have the following records as well as many other record types. These records can also be rented or purchased from Heritage Quest, Online at proquest,com/products-services/heritagequest.html, or at PO Box 329, Bountiful, Utah 84011-0329; (700) 760-2455.

49

Records are organized by Record Group, from smallest to largest:

- RECORD: a piece or item of information in any physical form (paper, photographic, motion picture tape, audio tape, computer tape, CD, etc.);
    - Example: A letter in a pension application file.
- FILE UNIT: Holds the records concerning the person, case, date or subject.
    - Example: Pension application file of an individual with supporting documents.
    - SERIES: Consist of File Units that deal with a particular subject, function or
    - activity, related by arrangement, source, use, physical form or action taken. Example: Series 1--Approved applications of wives; Series 2– Unapproved;
- SUB-GROUP: Contains 2 or more Series related by subject, activity and source; Example: Applications for same period, Sub-Groups Civil War and Later.
- RECORD GROUP: Sub-Groups are combined into Record Groups according to the origin of the Sub-Group material–often for the records of a Bureau. Example: Records of the Veterans Administration, Records Group 15.

YOUR FAMILY TREE. Whether you decide to make a simple Family Tree of immediate family members on both the maternal and paternal side of your family, or a complex, in-depth Genealogy or Pedigree Chart, **the photos and especially the stories you discover and save will make it interesting to other family members and future generations.**

YOUR PEDIGREE CHART. This is a more complex presentation of one's genealogy. The word "pedigree" is a corruption of the French "pied de grue" or crane's foot, because the typical lines and split lines (each split leading to different offspring of the one parent line) resemble the thin leg and foot of a crane. Pedigrees use a standardized set of symbols, squares represent males and circles represent females. It should be noted that pedigree construction is family history, and as such details about an earlier generation may be uncertain as memories fade. If the sex of the person is unknown a diamond is used. Someone with the phenotype in question is represented by a filled-in (darker) symbol. Heterozygotes, when identifiable, are indicated by a shade dot inside a symbol or a half-filled symbol.

Relationships in a pedigree are shown as a series of lines. Parents are connected by a horizontal line, and a vertical line leads to their offspring. The offspring are connected by a horizontal sibship line and listed in birth order from left to right. If the offspring are twins then they will be connected by a triangle. If an offspring dies then its symbol will be crossed by a line. If the offspring is stillborn or aborted it is represented by a small triangle. Each generation is identified by a Roman numeral (I, II, III, and so on), and each individual within the same generation is identified by an Arabic number (1, 2, 3, and so on). Analysis of the pedigree using the principles of Mendelian inheritance can determine whether a trait has a dominant or recessive pattern of inheritance. Pedigrees are often constructed after a family member afflicted with a genetic disorder has been identified. This individual, known as the proband, is indicated on the pedigree by an arrow.

If your research leads you to other countries, you can probably find genealogists who specialize in the country you'd like to have researched to find your ancestors and most often you won't be charged if the genealogist regards it as a hobby rather than a business. *The Ultimate Search Book – Worldwide Edition* includes resources in every state and 200 countries. Ancestry.com provides a simple fill-in-the blanks format for your name and name of one of your parents with any known information, then builds your Family Tree on both the paternal and maternal side.

NATIONAL CENSUS. A Census of the population has been taken every 10 years since 1790 and can be a useful resource for tracing your family tree. Microfilm copies are available for the 1790-1880 schedules, for surviving fragments of the 1890 census, and for the 1900-1940 schedules. Almost all of the 1890 Census was destroyed by fire in 1921. The remaining schedules for 1890 consist of small segments of the population of Perry County, AL; District of Columbia; Columbus, GA; Mound Township, IL; Rockford, MN; Jersey City, NJ; Eastchester and Brookhaven Township, NY; Cleveland and Gaston Counties, NC; Cincinnati and Wayne Township, OH; Jefferson Township, SD; and Ellis, Hood, Kauffman, Rusk and Trinity Counties, TX. The 1790-1840 schedules give the names of heads of household only; other family members are tallied unnamed by age and sex. For the 1850 and 1860 Censuses, separate schedules list slave owners and the age, sex and color (but not the name) of each slave, and the county of birth of each free person in the household. Additional information is included in each succeeding Census.The published censuses for 1790 are for Connecticut, Maine, Maryland, Massachusetts, New Hampshire, New York, North Carolina, and Vermont. Censuses for the remaining states–Delaware, Georgia, Kentucky, New Jersey, Tennessee and Virginia–were burned during the War of 1812. As a substitute, the federal government published names obtained from state censuses and tax lists, thereby listing over half the population of the state in 1790. Helpful in locating specific Census entries are the following unpublished indexes in the National Archives: 1810 Census – a card index for Virginia only; 1880 Census – a microfilm copy of a card index to entries for each household that included children under 10; 1890 Census – a card index to the 6,160 names of surviving schedules; 1900 Census – a microfilm copy of an index to heads of families; 1910 Census – a microfilm copy of an index to all heads of families in the following states: Alabama, Arkansas, California, Florida, Georgia, Illinois, Kansas, Kentucky, Louisiana, Michigan Mississippi, Missouri, North Carolina, Tennessee, Texas, Virginia, West Virginia. Also available on microfilm are the 1890 schedules of Union veterans and their widows in alphabetical order from Louisiana through Wyoming. Records are available relating to Indians who kept their tribal status, mostly 1830-1940. They include mainly Cherokee, Chickasaw, Choctaw and Creek, each of whom moved West during 1830-1846. Each entry on these lists usually contains the name of the head of the family, the number of persons in the family by age and sex, a description of the property owned before removal with the location of real property, and the dates of departure from the East and arrival in the West. The microfilm of the 1885 -1940 census rolls show each person in the family by their Indian or English name (or both), age, sex, relationship to head of family, sometimes their relationship to other enrolled Indians, and sometimes births and deaths during the year. The Census Bureau, established in 1902, is now located at 4600 Silver Hill Road, Prince George's Country, Suitland, MD 20746; (301) 763-5636. For specific information from the last Census, check the site map at the bottom of their home page at https://www.census.gov/# . For in-depth statistical and anecdotal research about adoptees, donor offspring and their related issues, "THE ADOPTION AND DONOR CONCEPTION FACTBOOK" is available in both Kindle and print book format on Amazon, or ask your local library to order it.

NATURALIZATION RECORDS. The Immigration and Naturalization Service (INS) has duplicate records of all naturalizations that occurred after September 26, 1906. Inquiries about citizenship granted after that date should be sent on a form available from INS district offices (address available from your local Postmaster).

GEN RING, PERSONAL FAMILY WEBSITES, MESSAGE BOARDS, GENEALOGY COLUMNS, NEWS GROUPS, DIRECTORIES, CHARTING SERVICES, COATS OF ARMS online can help you "branch out" in your search for your "roots."

- GenRing, web ring at wenring.org/hub/genring has over 1,000 genealogy websites.
- Public Profiler's World Names website at worldnames.publicprofiler.org/ will map the frequency of your name around the world, free.
- Cyndi's List at CyndisList.com has over 52,000 links in 100 categories, including free adoptee and parent reunion registries.
- Coats of Arms date back to the twelfth century. Frequently Asked Questions (and Answers) about Coats of Arms can be found at college-of-arms.gov.uk/resources/faqs

BOOKS FOR FURTHER RESEARCH. The Bibliography in the back section of this book provides both search-related books (those titles are bolded) and books by and about adoptees' and birthparents' experiences. GENEALOGICAL PUBLISHING COMPANY INC. and CLEARFIELD COMPANY, at Genealogical.com publishes genealogy books and CDs. Whether you are just beginning to explore your family tree or are an experienced researcher looking for in-depth genealogy data, Genealogical.com can provide you with the resources you need. They publish over 2,000 genealogy books and CDs featuring colonial genealogy, Irish genealogy, immigration, royal ancestry, family history, and genealogy methods and sources. "THE GENEALOGIST'S ADDRESS BOOK" by Elizabeth Petty Bentley, has national and state addresses for archives, libraries, historical societies, genealogical societies, ethnic and religious organizations, and "HISTORY FOR GENEALOGISTS" by Judy Jacobson, which uses chronological time lines for finding and understanding your ancestors. Heritage Quest, at is a publisher of genealogical books and materials and also offers a lending library at heritagequestonline.com/hqoweb/library/do/index/

The aforementioned books are also available on Amazon, at public libraries, or you can ask the Acquisitions Librarian at your local public or university library to order them for both their Reference shelves and for check out.

Chapter 6:
DEBTORS; DEADBEAT PARENTS; HEIRS; CLASSMATES;
OLD LOVES... or ANYONE

DEBTORS. Collection agencies in every city are able to pursue debtors for companies and individuals who are owed money, usually as result of being awarded a court judgment. Most do not charge up-front fees but will deduct a percentage, such as 50% of amounts if and when collected, according to a written agreement. The collections agency should offer the debtor the option of not having negative information placed on their credit report if they pay the debt promptly in full or in accordance with a monthly payment schedule. If you want to try to collect on your own, you must first make a written demand for payment by certified return-receipt mail, stating the maximum time in which the debtor must pay you or make arrangement for payments. If you cannot collect what is owed you, the next step is to file a claim in Small Claims Court and obtain a judgment. If the debtor owns or may in the future own real estate, it's a good idea to have the County Recorder record the judgment so that a lien can be placed against the property. If the debtor is employed, you can hire the local authority who can serve the employer with an order to garnish the person's wages for the amount owed, or, if you know where the person banks, you can have the authority serve the bank with an Order to garnish the account. If the debtor has filed for bankruptcy, the bankruptcy court determines the priority of claims if there is money to pay them.

DEADBEAT PARENTS.   There may be legitimate reasons for a parent to fall behind in child support payments, such as unemployment, which can be worked out by communicating, not avoiding the issue. But the parent will still owe any back child support payments missed, and in order to establish the parent's obligation, a court has to award a specific amount of child support to be paid until the child is of legal age. The child should have a Social Security Number and a child support payment account established. The District Attorney for the county in which the child support was incurred can sue the parent who owes child support and garnish their wages, place liens against property, and initiate legal prosecution to enforce court-ordered child support.

HEIRS. "Probate" is the legal determination by a Probate Court of the validity of a will. The Probate Court for the county in which the deceased maintained their "last legal residence" has jurisdiction and requires probate for estates over a certain amount (for instance, over $60,000). The court does not search for heirs. A Legal Death Notice and hearing must be published (usually by an attorney, administrator or executor) in a newspaper in the county of the last legal residence. A will usually designates an Executor or Administrator to carry out the deceased person's wishes. If a deceased relative or friend has named you as Administrator or Executor, you will have to locate any heirs if you don't already know where they are. If they are not listed in WhitePages.com or local directories, check online business directories for "Legal Services," "Locators" or similar listings for Heir Searchers who also advertise in the Martindale-Hubbell attorney directory at Martindale.com since lawyers will hire them to find an heir. It is important that attempts to locate and legally notify heirs be documented. As when hiring a detective, check references.

CLASSMATES.   Classmates.com and Reunions.com make it easy to find a former classmate if she or she has added their name to those on the website as they can be found by browsing those listed. However, one must pay a membership fee in order to contact someone via Classmates.com messaging. Classmates.com and public libraries may have the high school yearbook for the year that the person you seek graduated. Forthcoming high school reunions and updates are posted.

OLD LOVES.   People are often separated by circumstances such as war, distance, family or other relationships. We often hear about an older couple who haven't seen each other in decades and have re-kindled a past romance. They may have been married and divorced or widowed in the meantime, and may now be at a place in their lives where the relationship can be fulfilling.   This book provides all the ways that you can find anyone anywhere, even without knowing their current name to start. If you had originally met while in school, Classmates.com may provide their current whereabouts and a means for contact.   Depending on how much you knew and remember about the person, you might find them at the same job or business, or through mutual friends.   You may both, by coincidence, both be on Facebook.com, or a free date site, PlentyOfFish.com, or fee-based dating website such as Match.com, or OurTime.com for singles who are 50+.

C A U T I O N : Scammers also lurk on all date sites. As with any search for someone you haven't seen in a long time, one must be respectful of the other person's current situation and whether or not they are interested in meeting again.

Chapter 7:
STARTING YOUR OWN SEARCH BUSINESS

While it's been the policy of this author and her organization, Americans For Open Records (AmFOR), to not charge fees for search assistance, charging reasonable fees for one's work and actual expenses is certainly acceptable. There are two types of search businesses. One is the result of enjoying doing research to solve a case, just as one would have satisfaction from solving any puzzle. The other type results from a deep sense or moral conviction that "the system" is inadequate to serve the needs of those you can help with your services. *It's not illegal to search for one's family,* but in the case of adoptee and parent searches, the system creates roadblocks to prevent people from accessing records in which they are named, and from the freedom to choose whether to associate. Consequently, the people within the system sell them the information and contact with biological family members. In order to decide whether a search *business* would be of interest to you, complete a search – your own or a friend's – and become familiar with your local public records offices and their publicly accessed computers. Another way to find your niche is to work for a private investigator or an attorney who needs someone to do "skip tracing" and property searches on an hourly or flat fee per trace basis. The job of searching property files on computer or in file drawers at a county tax assessor's office, and civil and criminal records and dockets at courthouses or online, can be tedious, but the end result can be satisfying. After requiring experience as a skip tracer, researcher or searcher, you will have a better idea whether you want to spend your time on repetitive tasks, and are flexible enough to enjoy the challenge that each new case may present.

TIPS FOR DEVELOPING A SUCCESSFUL SEARCH BUSINESS.

STEP 1: TEST THE MARKET. After you've decided on a good name for your business; filed your fictitious name statement; obtained a business license; set up a business account; bought a computer and reliable Internet access; found out what others are charging for the same services and priced yours competitively; created a web page about your business with photos; made some inexpensive business cards that list your services, phone number, mailing address, email address and website, don't spend a lot of money for ads while just waiting for the phone to ring. Find and fill the needs of local attorneys, security companies, collections agencies, bail bondsmen, preferably by face to face contact and hand them your card. Look for individuals and adoptee groups on Facebook whose pages and newsfeeds state they are looking for someone.

STEP 2: NOTIFY OTHERS YOU EXIST – PROMOTE YOUR BUSINESS WITH A VIDEO TAPE featuring a human interest case you've solved and offering your help with other cases. Next upload the video to You Tube, being sure your phone number is prominently displayed.

STEP 3: BUILD YOUR REFERENCE LIBRARY. "BIZ OPS: STARTING, BUYING & SELLING BUSINESSES BIG OR SMALL" by Stanley Reyburn offers sound advice and resources at https:/Amazon.com/dp/B00BKA4DD4.

BIBLIOGRAPHY
(Note: Titles specifically related to searching are **bolded**)

Anderson, Laura, *"Baby of Mine: A Birthmother's Journey Through Forced Adoption,"* Kindle (Amazon), (2021)

Austin, Linda Tollet, *"Babies For Sale: The Tennessee Children's Home,"* Greenwood Press, (1993)

Bentley, Elizabeth Petty, ***"The Genealogist's Address Book - 6th Edition,"*** (812 pages), Genealogical Publishing Company, (2009)

Bertrand, Neal, ***"From Cradle to Grave: Journey of the Louisiana Orphan Train Riders,"*** Cypress Cove Publishing, (2014)

Block, William, ***"Advanced Private Investigation,"*** Information Today, (2001)

Blockson, Charles, ***"Black Genealogy,"*** Black Classic Press, (1991)

Bonneur, Christine, *"Losing Six Kids (My Failed Adoption Story),"* iUniverse, (2017)

Brodzinsky, David M., *"Being Adopted: The Lifelong Search for Self,"* Doubleday, (1992)

Burton, Bob, ***"Bail Enforcer: The Advanced Bounty Hunter,"*** Paladin Press, (1990)

Campbell, Lee H., PhD, *"Cast Off: They Called Us Dangerous Women,"* (2014); and *"Stow Away: They Told Me to Forget,"* CreateSource Independent Publishing, (2013)

Carp, E. Wayne, *"Jean Paton and the Struggle to Reform American Adoption,"* University of Michigan Press, (2014)

Chatelain, Maurice, *"Our Ancestors Came From Outer Space,"* Dell Publishing, (1991)

Clagett, Brice M., *"The Death of Genealogy,"* National Genealogical Society Newsletter, (February 1990)

Coles, Gary, *"Ever After: Fathers and the Impact of Adoption,"* Clova Publications, (2006)

Cox, Susan Soon-Keum, *"Voices From Another Place: A Collection of Works From a Generation Born in Korea and Adopted to Other Countries,"* Yeong & Yeong, (1999)

Department of Justice, ***"A Family Resource Guide on International Parental Kidnapping,"*** CreateSpace Independent Platform, (2012)

Easterly, Sara, *"Searching for Mom: A Memoir,"* Heart Values (Kindle), (2019)

Eldridge, Sherry, *"Twenty Things Adopted Kids Wished Their Adoptive Parents Knew,"* Dell Books, (1999)

Fessler, Ann, *"The Girls Who Went Away,"* Penguin Books, (2000)

Field, Joe, *"Finding Joe Adams: Overcoming Great Odds A Son Searches for His Father,"* Independently Published (Amazon), 2020

Gauthreaux, Alan G., *"Italian Louisiana: History, Heritage and Tradition,"* The History Press, (2014)

Glaser, Gabrielle, *"American Baby: A Mother, A Child and the Shadow History of Adoption,"* Viking, (2021)

Greenwood, Val D., ***"A Researcher's Guide to American Genealogy,"*** 3rd Edition, Genealogical Publishing Company, (2013)

Griffith, Keith C., *"The Right To Know Who You Are,"* Katherine Kinbell Publisher, (1992)

Heikkila, Kim, *"Booth Girls: Pregnancy, Adoption and the Secrets We Kept,"* Minnesota Historical Society Press, (2021)

Hentz, Trace L., *"Two Worlds: Lost Children of the Indian Adoption Project (Vol. 1, Second Edition,"* Blue Hand Books, (2017)

Hoffman. Michael, *"They Were White and They Were Slaves: The Untold History of the Enslavement of Whites in Early America,"* Independent History, (1993)

Jacobson, Judy, *"**History for Genealogists: Using Chronological Time Lines to Find and Understand Your Ancestors**,"* Clearfield Company for Genealogical Publishing, (2009)

Jones, Merry, *"Birthmothers: Women Who Have Relinquished Babies for Adoption Tell Their Stories,"* Open Road Distribution, (2016)

Katz, William Loren, *"The Black West: A Documentary and Pictorial History of the African American Role in the Western Expansion of the United States,"* Touchstone, (1996)

Krantz, Les, and Chris Smith, *"**The Unofficial Census**,"* Arcade Publishing, (2003)

Lifton, Betty, *"Journey of the Adopted Self: A Quest for Wholeness,"* Basic Books, (1995)

McGilvrey, Valerie, *"**Skip Trace Secrets: Dirty Little Tricks Skip Tracers Use**,"* CreateSpace Independent Platform, (2013)

Melanson, Yvette, and Claire Safran, *"Looking for Lost Bird: A Jewish Woman's Discovery of Her Navajo Roots,"* Harper Perennial, (2000)

Moreno, Barry, *"**Children of Ellis Island**,"* Arcadia Publishing, (2003)

Newton, Nancy, *"Primal Wound: Understanding Your Adopted Child,"* Gateway Press, (2003)

O'Connell, Alaina, *"Open. (An Adoption Story in Three Voices),"* Balboa Press, (2017)

Oh, Arissa H., *"To Save the Children: The Cold War Origins of International Adoption (Asian American),"* Stanford University Press, (2015)

Parr, KeLee, *"Mansion On A Hill: The Story of the Willows Maternity Sanitarium and the Adoption Hub of America,"* Independently Published (Amazon), (2018); *"And More Voices of the Willows,"* Bowker (2020)

Price, Gary, and Chris Sherman, *"**The Invisible Web: Uncovering Information Sources Search Engines Can't See**,"* Information Today, (2001)

Reyburn, Stanley, *"Biz Ops: Starting, Buying & Selling Businesses Big or Small,"* Access Press, 2019

Rimer, Kelly, *"The Secret Daughter: A Beautiful Novel of Adoption, Heartbreak and a Mother's Love,"* Bookouture, (2015)

Roorde, Ronda M., *"In Their Voices: Black Americans on Transracial Adoption,"* Columbia University Press, (2015)

Rose, James M., PhD, and Alice Eichholz, PhD, *"Black Genesis,"* Genealogical Publishing Company, (2008)

Ross, Andrea, *"Unnatural Selection: A Memoir of Adoption and Wilderness,"* CavanKerry Press, (2021)

Smolenyah, Megan, *"**Who Do You Think You Are?: The Essential Guide to Tracing Your Family History**,"* Penguin Books, (2010)

Simon, Rita J., *"In Their Own Voices: Transracial Adoptees Tell Their Stories,"* Columbia University Press (2000)

Smith, Franklin Carter, and Emily Ann Croom, *"**A Genealogist's Guide to Discovering Your African American Ancestors**,"* Genealogical Publishing, (2005)

Solinger, Rickie, *"Beggars and Choosers: How the Politics of Choice Shapes Adoption, Abortion and Welfare in the United States"* Holt and Wang, (2002); and *"Wake Up Little Susie: Single Pregnancy and Race Before Roe v. Wade,"* 2nd Edition, Routledge, (2000)

Soll, Joe, *"Adoption Healing: A Path to Recovery,"* Adoption Crossroads, 2nd Edition, (2020)

Sorosky, Arthur D., Annette Baran, et al, *" The Adoption Triangle,"* Triadoption Publications, (2008)

Springs, Karen, *"Adoption Through the Rear View Mirror: Learning From Stories of Heartache and Hope,"* Forward Reflections, (2020)

Thomas, Gordon, *"Enslaved: The Chilling Modern-Day Abduction and Trafficking of Men, Women and Children,"* Pharos Books, (1991)

Von Danekin, Erich, *"Chariots of the Gods,"* Berkeley Press, (1990); and   *"History is Wrong,"* New Page Books, (2012)

Wenzel, Rosemary, ***"Tracing Your Jewish Ancestors - Second Edition: A Guide for Family and Historians,"*** Pen and Sword (2014)

Werner, Emma E*., "Passage to America: Oral Histories of Child Immigrants from Ellis Island,"* Potomac Books, (2009)

Wheeler, Joan M., *"Forbidden Family,"* Trafford Publishing, (2009)

Wilson-Buterbaugh, Karen, *"The Baby Scoop Era,"* Amazon (2017)

DIRECTORY of RESOURCES and WEBSITES - by Subject

ADOPTEE, BIRTHPARENT, SIBLING SEARCH, SUPPORT GROUPS, PIs (See also REUNION REGISTRIES)

ALMA SOCIETY (Adoptees Liberty Movement Association) - almasociety.org/

AMERICAN ADOPTION CONGRESS (AAC) (umbrella of Paid Search Groups and Activists) americanadoptioncongress.org

BASTARD NATION (BN) bastards.org

CONCERNED UNITED BIRTHPARENTS (CUB) - CuBirthparents.org

EMERGENCY, LIFE OR DEATH SEARCH (Volunteers, when available) ties-search.org email: l TIES@absnw.com

PRIVATE INVESTIGATION NETWORK P.I. MALL - pimall.com/

SEARCH ANGELS (Free) at THE SEEKER the-seeker.com/angels.htm ON FACEBOOK facebook.com/pages/Adoption-Free-Search-Angels/156749834387458 AND OTHERS adoption.com

ADOPTION AND FOSTER CARE DATA

THE ADOPTION AND DONOR CONCEPTION FACTBOOK (Paperback & Kindle available on Amazon

CHILD WELFARE INFORMATION GATEWAY (Federal Government website) childwelfare.gov/

CHOSEN CHILDREN (A Documentary) Available on Amazon.com

ADOPTION REFORM LEGISLATON, ACTIVISTS & ABOLITIONIST GROUPS

ADOPTION ACTIVISTS THINKING OUTSIDE THE BOX facebook.com/groups/

ADOPTIVE PARENTS FOR OPEN RECORDS & AGAINST ADOPTION Facebook.com/Anti-AdoptionAdopters

AMERICANS FOR OPEN RECORDS (AmFOR) https://www.facebook.com/AmFOR.net/

BASTARD NATION bastards.org/

FACEBOOK GROUPS facebook.com/groups/anti.adoption/ ?notif_t=group_r2j_approved ; Facebook.com/AbolishAdoption ; facebook.com/groups/35338433808147

DNA/GENETIC TESTING AND MATCHING SERVICES

ANCESTRY.COM
(Autosomal and Y-Chromosome)
-Ancestry.com

CABRI DONOR GAMETE ARCHIVE
(Male & Female, X/Y Chromosome DNA)
Connects half-siblings/donors for offspring
using X/Y chromosome testing;
Can only connect siblings of the same sex;
females must have mother tested]
cabrimed.org/donorconceivedservices.jsp

DNA DATABASES
isogg.org/wiki/DNA_databases

DNA TESTS (Autosomal) -
23andme.com

FAMILY TREE DNA (Autosomal) -
FamilyTreeDNA.com

UPLOAD DNA TEST RESULTS
(only from 23andMe) -
GEDMatch.com

Y-SEARCH Y-DNA PUBLIC DATABASE
(Male only, Y chromosome DNA)
Pro: Can identify paternal genetic surname,
giving male offspring an idea as to their
biological father's possible last name
Con: Because of infidelity/secret adoption and
donor-conception in direct line, genetic surname
may not be same as biological father's surname
Ysearch.org

DONOR OFFSPRING, SIBLING RESOURCES - REGISTRIES, FORUMS, SOCIAL NETWORKS

AMERICAN ASSOCIATION OF TISSUE
BANKS
aatb.org

AMERICAN SOCIETY FOR
REPRODUCTIVE MEDICINE (ASRM)
asrm.org

CHICAGO WOMEN'S HEALTH CENTER
(BANK)
chicagowomenshealthcenter.org

CRYOBANK's SIBLING REGISTRY
sibling-registry.com/howtoregister.cfm ;
nwcryobank.com/sign-in/?message=sign-
inrequired

DONOR CHILDREN
donorchildren.com ;
donorchildren.com/sample-page/getstarted

DONOR CONCEIVED REGISTER (UK)
http://donorconceivedregister.org.uk

DONOR CONCEPTION (Pre-1991)
fairfaxcryobank.com

DONORLINK (UK) (National Voluntary
Info Exchange and Contact Register
ukdonorlink.org.uk

DONOR OFFSPRING GROUP
http://DonorOffspring.com

DONOR OFFSPRING HEALTH PAGE
donoroffspringhealth.com

DONOR OFFSPRING RESEARCH PROJECT
(participation invited)
donorfamilyresearch.com

DONOR SIBLING REGISTRY (DSR)
(Fee for access; Wendy Kramer)
donorsiblingregistry.com

EVERYTHING SURROGACY -
Directories for Surrogacy Agencies, Egg
Donation Services, Attorneys, IVF
everythingsurrogacy.com

FAIRFAX CRYOBANK REGISTRIES
fairfaxcryobank.com

MIDWEST SPERM BANK
midwestspermbank.com

PEOPLE CONCEIVED BY ARTIFICIAL
INSEMINATION (PCVAI)
health.groups.yahoo.com/group/

SEARCHING FOR MY SPERM DONOR
FATHER
(Australia/US/UK/Canada profiles)
searchingformyspermdonorfather.or
g/country/Canada/

SPERM DONOR GROUP
health.groups.yahoo.com/group/Sperm
Donors/?yguid=3457069 ;
hdonorsiblinggroups.com/Donor_
Sibling_Group_Registr.php

KNOWN DONOR REGISTRY
KnownDonorRegistry.com

Y CONNECTIONS REGISTRY (Australia) -
donorconnections.com
/
[See also DNA/GENETC TESTING AND
MATCHING SERVICES]

GENEALOGY RESOURCES

ANCESTRY.com
Ancestry.com

BIOGRAPHIES FOR GENEALOGY
geneabios.com/

CYNDI'S LIST
cyndislist.com/

FAMILY TREE BUILDER
myheritage.com

FIND A GRAVE
Internment.net
NATIONWIDE GRAVE LOCATOR
Gravelocator.va.gov

GENEALOGICAL PUBLISHING
(FOR SPECIFIC SUBJECT, COUNTRY)
Genealogical.com

GENWEB
U.S. GENWEB PROJECT
usgenweb.org/

ROOTSWEB
rootsweb.ancestry.com/cgibin/igm.cgi

WORLDGENWEB
worldgenweb.org/countryindex.html

INTERNATIONAL GENEALOGICAL
INDEX
familysearch.org/search?PAGE=igi/search_
IGI.asp

SOCIAL SECURITY DEATH INDEX
genealogy.about.com/od/free_genealogy/a/s
sdi.htm

SORTED BY NAME
sortedbyname.com/index.html

MISSING CHILDREN

NATIONAL CENTER FOR MISSING &
EXPLOITED CHILDREN (NCMEC)
missingkids.com

PRISONER LOCATOR

PRISONER LOCATOR, BY STATE (Free)
ancdestorhunt.com/prison)search.htm

CALIFORNIA PRISONER LOCATOR
inmatelocator.cdcr.cagov (Free)

PUBLIC RECORDS DATABASE

searchsystems.net

REUNION REGISTRIES

ADOPTION DATABASE - REGISTRIES
adoptiondatabase.quickbase.com/db/bbqm9
4vvd

INTERNATIONAL SOUNDEX
REUNION
REGISTRY (ISRR) - (Free)
isrr.org; http://isrr,org/Register.html

MILITARY SEARCH
searchmil.com

SEARCH DIRECTORIES PEOPLE SEARCH, DOB SEARCH, REVERSE LOOKUPS, BIRTH INDEX, DEATH INDEX

WhitePages.com
AnyWho.com
411.com
SearchGateway.com (Free)
PeopleSearch.com (Fees apply)
Intelius.com (Fees apply)
Facebook.com
MySpace.com
Classmates.com
Reunions.com
DOBSEARCH.com

BIRTH INDEXES -
Visit you local FAMILY HISTORY
CENTER to view microfilm Birth Indexes
DEATH INDEX
Rootweb.com
ancestry.com/search

RANCH HANDS DATABASE
searches.rootsweb.com

SUBJECT SEARCH ONLINE.
LIBRARIAN'S INDEX TO THE
INTERNET
sunsite.berkeley.edu/InternetIndex

ULTIMATE SEARCH BOOK, THE -
(WORLDWIDE EDITION and
U.S. EDITION, e-book & print edition)
Available on Amazon.com

WORLDWIDE PHONE DIRECTORIES
Phonebookoftheworld

SEPARATED UNACCOMPANIED MIGRANT CHILDREN AND FAMILIES

OFFICE OF REFUGEE RESETTLEMENT (ORR)
to locate separated migrant kids/families
1-800-203-7001
information@ORRNCC.com
Administration for Children & Families -
Switzer Building,
330 C St SW, Room 5123
Washington, DC 20201
Ph: 202-401-9246; fax 202-401-1022

ADDENDUM
BIRTH CERTIFICATES AND RELATED FORMS

(1)   **Hospital Issued Birth Certificate** (Connecticut)

(2)   **3 State Health Department Issued Birth Certificates/Registration** (Connecticut)

(3)   **State Vital Records Issued Birth Certificate** (Connecticut)

(4)   **Short Form** (Coupon Size) **Certificate** (Connecticut)

(5)   **Original** (True) **Long Form Birth Certificate** *Biological Parents on Date of Birth* (CT)

(6)   **Amended** (Falsified) **Birth Certificate** *Adoptive Parents As Parents on DOB* (CT)

(7)   **Adoptee's Original Army Base Hospital Issued Provided To Adoptee**,

(8)   **Adoption Decree**, Unblocked (Washington State)

(9)   **Adoption Certificate** (Unofficial, created by an adoptive mother)

(10)   **Waiver Of Confidentiality For "Birth" Mothers** (Generic for any state)

(11)   **Waiver Of Confidentiality For Siblings** (California)

(12)   **Consent For Contact For "Birth" Parent or Adoptee (California)**

(13)   **International Soundex Reunion Registry** (ISRR) Registration Form (Page 1)

(14)   **International Soundex Reunion Registry** (ISRR) Registration Form (Page 2)

(15)   **Request To Waive Court Fees** (California)

(16)   **U.S. State Department Issued Apostille Birth** (California, Connecticut)

(17)   **Hospital Record Of Newborn's Footprints Thumb And Finger Prints**

(18)   **Certified Nurse Midwife** (CNM) **Home Birth & Midwife License** (Illinois)

(19)   **County Issued Birth Certificate** (Cook County, Illinois)

(20)   **City Issued Birth Certificate** (Chicago, Illinois)

(21)   **Catholic Birth And Baptism Certificate**

(22)   **Jewish Birth Certificate/Child's Hebrew/Circumcision Certificate** (New York)

(23)   **Mormon Birth Certificate From Record At Chihuahua, Mexico** (Utah)

(24)   **"Sex Not Specified" Birth Certificate** (Australia)

(25)   **3 Parent (LGBT) And Transgender Birth Certificates** (Florida and California)

(1) HOSPITAL ISSUED BIRTH CERTIFICATE
(Connecticut)

The Hospital of Saint Raphael

Certificate of Birth

This Certifies that _____ was born to _____ in this Hospital at _____ the _____ day of _____ A. D. 19__

In Witness Whereof the said Hospital has caused this Certificate to be signed by its duly authorized officer and its Official Seal to be hereunto affixed.

STATE OF CONNECTICUT   DEPARTMENT OF HEALTH

Birth Certificate

This is to certify that

Herbert Brandage 3nd

was born in Stratford Conn. on October 3, 1920

Father's name Herbert Brandage Jr.

Mother's maiden name Beatrice Lucia Mandell

The full record of this birth has been carefully filed and is preserved in the archives of the State of Connecticut.

EVERY MOTHER IS ENTITLED TO A BIRTH CERTIFICATE FOR HER CHILD.

STATE OF CONNECTICUT   DEPARTMENT OF HEALTH

Notice of Registration of Birth

This is to certify that

Lorraine Carangelo   92 Carmel Street

was born April 3, 1945 in Hospital of St.Raphael New Haven, Conn.

Father's name Alfred B. Carangelo

Mother's maiden name Anna Delcesqua

The full record of this birth has been carefully filed and is preserved in the archives of the State of Connecticut.

EVERY MOTHER IS ENTITLED TO A NOTICE OF REGISTRATION OF BIRTH OF HER CHILD

Bureau of Vital Statistics	CONNECTICUT STATE DEPARTMENT OF HEALTH	Certificate of Birth

1. Place of Birth: New Haven, Conn.
a. County New Haven, Conn.
b. City or Town New Haven, Conn.
c. Name of Hospital or Institution St.Raphael's Hosp.
   Note: If not in hospital or institution, give street No. or location

d. Length of mother's stay before delivery: in hospital or institution 1 day
   In this community 17 yrs.

4. Full name of child Lorraine Carangelo

4. Date of birth Apr. 3, 1945
   month day year

5. Sex female

FATHER OF CHILD

8. Full name Alfred B. Carangelo
Residence New Haven, Conn.

9. Race white   10. Age 40

11. Birthplace New Haven, Conn.
   City or town   State or foreign country

12. Usual occupation High Standard

13. Place of occupation

14. Social Security Number

22. Other Children born to this mother:
(a) How many other children of this mother are now living? 0
(b) How many other children were born alive but are now dead? 0
(c) How many children were born dead? 0

24. I hereby certify that I attended the birth of this child; who was born alive at the hour of 3:59aM. on the date above stated and that the information given was furnished by mother related to this child as

25. Date on which given name added on supplemental report

By _____ Registrar

Form 0-VS 16 Rev. (7-44) 40M

---

2. Usual residence of mother:
a. State
b. County New Haven, Conn.
c. City or town

d. Street No. 92 Carmel St.

6. Twin or triplet?
   If so, born 1st, 2nd, 3rd?

7. Number months of pregnancy 9

MOTHER OF CHILD

15. Full maiden name Anna Delcesqua

16. Race white   17. Age 30

18. Birthplace New York City, New York
   City or town   State or foreign country

19. Usual occupation housewife

20. Place of occupation

21. Social Security Number

23. Mother's mailing address for registration notice Above

Was blood test made? yes
Date 2-45
If not made, give reason

Attendant's own signature S. Capobiatro,
Specify if physician, midwife, or other M.D.
Date Signed 4-5-45
Address New Haven, Conn.

THE SEAL OF THE STATE DEPARTMENT OF HEALTH SERVICES IS AFFIXED TO CERTIFY THAT THE ABOVE IS A TRUE COPY OF A RECORD FILED WITH THE DEPARTMENT OF HEALTH SERVICES PURSUANT TO THE PROVISIONS OF THE GENERAL STATUTES OF CONNECTICUT.

Douglas S. Lloyd, M.D.
Commissioner of Health Services

SEP 1 2 1983

Registrar of Vital Records

(3) STATE ISSUED BIRTH CERTIFICATE
(California)

STATE OF CALIFORNIA
DEPARTMENT OF HEALTH SERVICES

CERTIFICATE OF DEATH
STATE OF CALIFORNIA
USE BLACK INK ONLY AMENDED 1 OF 2

LOCAL REGISTRATION DISTRICT AND CERTIFICATE NUMBER
3-91-30-013733

STATE FILE NUMBER	1A. NAME OF DECEDENT—FIRST (GIVEN) Helen	1B. MIDDLE Isabel	1C. LAST (FAMILY) Engstrom

2A. DATE OF DEATH—MO, DAY, YR: December 23, 1991 — 2B. HOUR 0905 — SEX F

DECEDENT PERSONAL DATA

4. RACE White	5. HISPANIC—SPECIFY [X] No	6. DATE OF BIRTH—MO, DAY, YR November 11, 1913	7. AGE IN YEARS 78
8. STATE OF BIRTH NY	9. CITIZEN OF WHAT COUNTRY U.S.A.	10A. FULL NAME OF FATHER Emmett McCord Manning	10B. STATE OF BIRTH IA
11A. FULL MAIDEN NAME OF MOTHER Elizabeth Vass			11B. STATE OF BIRTH NY
12. MILITARY SERVICE	13. SOCIAL SECURITY NO. 520-30-7216	14. MARITAL STATUS Widowed	15. NAME OF SURVIVING SPOUSE IF WIFE, ENTER MAIDEN NAME None
16A. USUAL OCCUPATION Bridge Teacher	16B. USUAL KIND OF BUSINESS OR INDUSTRY Education	16C. USUAL EMPLOYER Arizona State Colleg	16D. YEARS IN OCCUPATION 30

17. EDUCATION—YEARS COMPLETED 12

USUAL RESIDENCE

18A. RESIDENCE—STREET AND NUMBER OR LOCATION 24882 Stem	18B. CITY El Toro	18C. ZIP CODE 92630
18D. COUNTY Orange	18E. NUMBER OF YEARS IN THIS COUNTY 3	18F. STATE OR FOREIGN COUNTRY CA

20. NAME, RELATIONSHIP, MAILING ADDRESS AND ZIP CODE OF INFORMANT
Linda E. Rehart - daughter
24882 Stem
El Toro, CA 92630

PLACE OF DEATH

19A. PLACE OF DEATH Saddleback Memorial Med. Ctr.	19B. IF HOSPITAL SPECIFY ONE IP	19C. COUNTY Orange
19D. STREET ADDRESS—STREET AND NUMBER OR LOCATION 24451 Health Center Drive	19E. CITY Laguna Hills	

22. WAS DEATH REPORTED TO CORONER? [X] No

CAUSE OF DEATH

21. DEATH WAS CAUSED BY: ENTER ONLY ONE CAUSE PER LINE FOR A, B, AND C	TIME INTERVAL BETWEEN ONSET AND DEATH	23. WAS BIOPSY PERFORMED?
IMMEDIATE CAUSE (A) Sepsis	1 day	[X] No
DUE TO (B) Bowel Infarction	1 day	24. WAS AUTOPSY PERFORMED? [X] No
DUE TO (C) Atherosclerosis	years	24B. WAS IT USED IN DETERMINING CAUSE OF DEATH? No

25. OTHER SIGNIFICANT CONDITIONS CONTRIBUTING TO DEATH BUT NOT RELATED TO CAUSE GIVEN IN 21
Congestive heart failure, Atrial Fibrillation

26. WAS OPERATION PERFORMED FOR ANY CONDITION IN ITEM 21 OR 25? IF YES, LIST TYPE OF OPERATION AND DATE. No

PHYSICIAN'S CERTIFICATION

27A. DECEDENT ATTENDED SINCE — MONTH, DAY, YEAR 12/22/91
27A. DECEDENT LAST SEEN ALIVE — MONTH, DAY, YEAR 12/22/91

27B. [signature]
27C. PHYSICIAN'S LICENSE NUMBER G49797
27D. DATE SIGNED 12/23/91

27E. TYPE ATTENDING PHYSICIAN'S NAME AND ADDRESS
Gregory S. Thomas, M.D., 26732 Crown Valley Parkway., Mission Viejo, CA 92692

CORONER'S USE ONLY

28. MANNER OF DEATH	30A. PLACE OF INJURY	30B. INJURY AT WORK	30C. DATE OF INJURY	31. HOUR

30D. LOCATION (STREET AND NUMBER OR LOCATION AND CITY)

32. DESCRIBE HOW INJURY OCCURRED (EVENTS WHICH RESULTED IN INJURY)

FUNERAL DIRECTOR AND LOCAL REGISTRAR

34A. DISPOSITION(S) TR/BU	34B. PLACE OF FINAL DISPOSITION—NAME AND ADDRESS Lakeview Cemetery., Cheyenne, WY	34C. DATE—MO, DAY, YEAR Dec. 26, 1991	35A. SIGNATURE OF EMBALMER [signature]	35B. LICENSE NUMBER 4641
36A. NAME OF FUNERAL DIRECTOR OR PERSON ACTING AS SUCH Eackes-Kailbers Baggott & Schacht	36B. LICENSE NO. FD-194	37. [signature] R. Rey Elling, D E Mezzyd		38. REGISTRATION DATE DEC 24 1991

STATE REGISTRAR

A.	B.	C.	D.	E.	CENSUS TRACT

05-11 (REV. 9-91)

MAKE NO ERASURES, WHITEOUTS, OR OTHER ALTERATIONS

(4) SHORT FORM (COUPON SIZE) BIRTH CERTIFICATE
(Connecticut)

CERTIFICATION OF BIRTH

STATE OF CONNECTICUT
DEPARTMENT OF PUBLIC HEALTH

Vital Records Section, Hartford, Connecticut, U.S.A.

Registration No. 106-91-16272

Name RACHEL ELIZABETH SOLLECITO

Date of Birth May 23, 1991 Sex Female

Place of Birth New Britain, CT

Reg. Date 6/4/1991 Date Issued 12/8/2010

This is a True Certification of Name and Birth Facts
as Recorded in this Office

By *Maria James, asst*

Local Registrar of Vital Statistics

Town of New Britain

STATE OF CONNECTICUT

69

(5) ORIGINAL (TRUE) LONG FORM BIRTH CERTIFICATE NAMING BIOLOGICAL PARENTS ON DATE OF BIRTH
(Connecticut)

CONNECTICUT STATE DEPARTMENT OF HEALTH

Public Health Statistics Section — Hartford, Connecticut, U.S.A.

Certificate of Birth

REGISTRATION NO. 105-68 **46563**

1. PLACE OF BIRTH: (a) State of Connecticut	2. USUAL RESIDENCE OF MOTHER: (a) State **Conn.**	
(b) County / (c) Town	(b) County / (c) Town	(d) Is Residence Inside a City or Borough Limits?
New Haven / New Haven	New Haven / Hamden	Yes ☐ No ☐ If Yes, name City or Borough

(d) Name of Hospital or Institution (if not in a hospital or institution, give Street No. or location): **Hospital of St. Raphael**

(e) Street Number (If rural, give location): **201 Augur Street**

3. CHILD'S NAME (First) (Middle) (Last) (Type or Print): **Richard Marotti**

4. DATE OF BIRTH (Month)(Day)(Year): **December 17, 1968**

5. SEX: **Male** / 6. (a) THIS BIRTH: Single ☒ Twin ☐ Triplet ☐ / (b) IF TWIN OR TRIPLET, WAS CHILD BORN 1st ☐ 2nd ☐ 3rd ☐

7. (a) LENGTH OF PREGNANCY WEEKS: **38** / (b) WEIGHT AT BIRTH COMPLETED: **6 lb. 15 oz.**

FATHER OF CHILD

8. FULL NAME: **Anthony P. Marotti**

9. RESIDENCE: **201 Augur Street, Hamden, Conn.**

10. RACE: **White** / 11. AGE AT TIME OF THIS BIRTH: **26**

12. BIRTHPLACE (City or town) (State or foreign country): **New Haven Conn.**

13. USUAL OCCUPATION: **Drill press operator**

14. INDUSTRY OR BUSINESS: **Unknown**

20. (a) WAS BLOOD TEST MADE? (Yes or No) **Yes** / (b) Date of test **6-11-68** / (c) If blood test not made, reason why not

MOTHER OF CHILD

15. FULL MAIDEN NAME: **Lorraine Carangelo**

16. RACE: **White** / 17. AGE AT TIME OF THIS BIRTH: **23**

18. BIRTHPLACE (City or town) (State or foreign country): **New Haven Conn.**

19. PREVIOUS PREGNANCY HISTORY OF THIS MOTHER (Do NOT include this birth):
(a) How many other children of this mother are now living? **0**
(b) How many other children were born alive but are now dead? **1**
(c) How many children were born dead? (Products of conception, fetuses, born dead at ANY time after conception) **0**

21. MOTHER'S MAILING ADDRESS: **201 Augur Street, Hamden, Conn.**

22. I HEREBY CERTIFY that I attended the birth of this child who was born alive at the hour of **1:12a** m. on the date above stated and that the information given was furnished by **Lorraine Marotti** related to this child as **Mother**

23. (a) ATTENDANT'S OWN SIGNATURE: *George H. Bonner, M.D.* **George E. Bonner, M.D.** / (b) Date Signed **12-16-68**

(c) Address: *111 Sherman Ave, New Haven, Conn 06511*

24. DATE ON WHICH GIVEN NAME WAS ADDED

BY _____ REGISTRAR

THIS CERTIFICATE RECEIVED FOR RECORD ON **DEC 23 1968**

BY *Gaetano Masella* REGISTRAR

Form VS-2

I certify that this is a true transcript of the information in this office.

Michael V. Lynch

Michael V. Lynch, Registrar
Carol Longobardi, Deputy Registrar
Maria DeGaetano, Ass't Registrar

Dated at New Haven, Connecticut, U.S.A., this **27** day of **NOVEMBER**, 1996

NOT VALID WITHOUT SEAL.

(6) AMENDED (FALSIFIED) BIRTH CERTIFICATE
NAMING ADOPTIVE PARENTS AS PARENTS ON DATE OF BIRTH
(Connecticut)

CONNECTICUT STATE DEPARTMENT OF HEALTH

Public Health Statistics Section — Hartford, Connecticut 06115, U. S. A.

46563

Certificate of Birth

1. PLACE OF BIRTH: (a) State of Connecticut	2. USUAL RESIDENCE OF MOTHER: (a) State Connecticut	
(b) County **New Haven** (c) Town **New Haven**	(b) County **New Haven** (d) Town **Meriden**	(d) Is Residence Inside City or Borough Limits? Yes ☐ No ☐ If Yes, name City or Borough
(d) Name of Hospital or Institution (If not in hospital or institution, give Street No. or location) **Hospital of Saint Raphael**	(e) Street Number (If rural, give location) **35 Sylvan Avenue**	

3. CHILD'S NAME (First) **Thomas** (Middle) **William** (Last) **Schafrick**	4. DATE OF BIRTH (Month) (Day) (Year) **December 17, 1968**	
5. SEX **Male**	6. (a) THIS BIRTH Single ☒ Twin ☐ Triplet ☐ (b) IF TWIN OR TRIPLET, WAS CHILD BORN 1ST ☐ 2ND ☐ 3RD ☐	7. (a) LENGTH OF PREGNANCY COMPLETED WEEKS **6** (b) WEIGHT AT BIRTH lb. **15** oz.

FATHER OF CHILD	MOTHER OF CHILD
8. FULL NAME **William Arthur Schafrick**	15. FULL MAIDEN NAME **Lois Edna Waller**
9. RESIDENCE **Meriden, Connecticut**	16. RACE **White** — 17. AGE AT TIME OF THIS BIRTH **27**
10. RACE **White** — 11. AGE AT TIME OF THIS BIRTH **29**	18. BIRTHPLACE (City or town) (State or foreign country) **Connecticut**
12. BIRTHPLACE (City or town) (State or Foreign country) **Connecticut**	19. PREVIOUS PREGNANCY HISTORY (a) How many other children of this mother are now living? **0**
13. USUAL OCCUPATION **Landscaper**	(b) How many other children were born alive but are now dead? **0**
14. INDUSTRY OR BUSINESS **Landscaping**	(Do NOT include this birth.) (c) How many children were born dead? **0**
20. (a) WAS BLOOD TEST MADE? (Yes or No) **—** (b) Date of test **—**	(Products of conception, fetuses, born dead at ANY time after conception)
(c) If blood test not made, reason why not **—**	21. MOTHER'S MAILING ADDRESS **35 Sylvan Avenue Meriden, Connecticut**

22. I HEREBY CERTIFY that I attended the birth of this child who was born alive at the hour of **1:12a** m. on the date above stated and that the information given was furnished by ____ related to this child as ____

23. (a) ATTENDANT'S OWN SIGNATURE **George A. Bonner, M.D.**	(b) Date Signed **December 16, 1968**
(c) Address **111 Sherman Avenue, New Haven, Connecticut**	

24. DATE ON WHICH GIVEN NAME ADDED	By	REGISTRAR
THIS CERTIFICATE RECEIVED FOR RECORD ON **December 23, 1968**	By	REGISTRAR **Gaetano Masella**

Form V.S. 51-8   4-70 3M

I certify that this is a true transcript of the information in this office.

Michael V. Lynch

Michael V. Lynch, Registrar
Carol Longobardi, Deputy Registrar
Maria DeGaetano, Ass't Registrar

Dated at New Haven, Connecticut, U.S.A., this **27** day of **NOVEMBER**, 1996

NOT VALID WITHOUT SEAL

71

(7) ADOPTEE'S ORIGINAL ARMY BASE HOSPITAL BIRTH CERTIFICATE BLOCKED, AS "NON-IDENTIFYNG INFORMATON"
(Hawaii)

STATE OF HAWAII	CERTIFICATE OF LIVE BIRTH	DEPARTMENT OF HEALTH

FILE NUMBER 1████ **63** ████

1a. Child's First Name (Type or print)	1b. Middle Name	1c. Last Name
ALAN		████

2. Sex	3. This Birth	4. If Twin or Triplet, Was Child Born	5a. Birth Date	Month	Day	Year	5b. Hour
Male	Single ☒ Twin ☐ Triplet ☐	1st ☐ 2nd ☐ 3rd ☐		██ber █		1963	█:47 A M.

6a. Place of Birth: City, Town or Rural Location	6b. Island
Honolulu	Oahu

6c. Name of Hospital or Institution (If not in hospital or institution, give street address)	6d. Is Place of Birth Inside City or Town Limits? If no, give judicial district
U. S. Army Tripler General Hospital	Yes ☒ No ☐

7a. Usual Residence of Mother: City, Town or Rural Location	7b. Island	7c. County and State or Foreign Country
Wahiawa	Oahu	Honolulu, Hawaii

7d. Street Address	7e. Is Residence Inside City or Town Limits? If no, give judicial district
████ Drive	Yes ☒ No ☐

7f. Mother's Mailing Address	7g. Is Residence on a Farm or Plantation?
	Yes ☐ No ☒

8. Full Name of Father	9. Race of Father
████	Caucasian

10. Age of Father	11. Birthplace (Island, State or Foreign Country)	12a. Usual Occupation	12b. Kind of Business or Industry
24		Officer	U. S. Army

13. Full Maiden Name of Mother	14. Race of Mother
████	Caucasian

15. Age of Mother	16. Birthplace (Island, State or Foreign Country)	17a. Type of Occupation Outside Home During Pregnancy	17b. Date Last Worked
22		School Teacher	10 Apr 63

I certify that the above stated information is true and correct to the best of my knowledge.	18a. Signature of Parent or Other Informant	Parent ☒ Other ☐	18b. Date of Signature 6 Sept 63
I hereby certify that this child was born alive on the date and hour stated above.	19a. Signature of Attendant ██ CAPT, MC, USA	M.D. ☒ D.O. ☐ Midwife ☐ Other ☐	19b. Date of Signature 6 Sept 63
20. Date Accepted by Local Reg. 6 Sept 63	21. Signature of Local Registrar ██ LT COL, MSC, USA		22. Date Accepted by Reg. General SEP 10 1963

23. Evidence for Delayed Filing or Alteration

(8) ADOPTION DECREE (UNBLOCKED)
(Washington state)

SUPERIOR COURT OF THE STATE OF WASHINGTON FOR CLARK COUNTY

In the Matter of the Adoption	NO. 04 5 00424 6
of	DECREE FOR ADOPTION
CHANCHAL,	
A Minor Child.	

THIS MATTER having come on regularly this day on the Petition of SCOTT JACKSON DONWERTH and MAYLA DAWN DONWERTH, husband and wife, for the adoption of CHANCHAL, and the Petitioners and the above named minor child appearing in person and by their attorney, and it appearing that Children's Hope International, the agency appointed by the Court to prepare the Postplacement Report, has filed said report, and the Court being fully advised in the premises, and having heard the evidence, and findings of fact and conclusions of law having been previously entered by the Court:

ADOPTION SUMMARY

1. The full original name of the person being adopted is CHANCHAL.

2. The new name of the person being adopted is AYANNA CHANCHAL DONWERTH

3. The adoptee's actual date of birth is May 7, 2003.

4. The adoptee's place of birth is the Country of India.

---

1 – DECREE FOR ADOPTION

Law Office of David R. Duncan
Post Office Box 5734
Vancouver, Washington 98668
(360) 816-1400
Fax: (360) 816-1100

73

(9) ADOPTION CERTIFICATE (UNOFFICIAL)
Created by an Adoptive Mother

Certificate of Adoption

This is to Certify that

MELISSIA ANNE GOODHEART

Has Been Formally Adopted

Into the Allman Family by the Mother Linda

and is Entitled to all the Rights and Privileges there to as One of Her Kids

ON THIS 1ST DAY OF JULY 2005

Linda J. Allman
Foster Mother

Philip E. Abbott
Senior Administrator

(10) WAIVER OF CONFIDENTIALITY for "BIRTH" MOTHERS
(Generic for Any State)

Dated: _____

TO: (Address it to Child and Family Services or similar public adoption agency, or to private adoption agency or attorney, where adoption was finalized and adoption file is held)

REF: My Name in full: _____

    Relinquished Child's Name at birth _____

    Child's Date and Place of Birth _____

    Relinquished/Placed for Adoption (on or about): _____

RE: NOTICE AND WAIVER OF CONFIDENTIALITY - TO ALL CONCERNED

I, _____, hereby formally request that this Notice and of my Waiver of Confidentiality not guaranteed to me by any laws or agencies in the state of _____ and/or copies hereof be immediately placed in all records and files pertaining to my above-referenced adoption. This Waiver of Confidentiality applies to all court records, hospital and other records of birth and medical history, and anything that may ve considered to be identifying information. I hereby also request non-identifying information about my relinquished child and would like to know whether there is any correspondence in the record intended for me or for my relinquished child.

The effects of this Waiver extend only to my "birth" child and/or my "birth" child's legal representatives. The following information may be released in full to the aforementioned parties: My name in full, my current address and phone number (shown below), any and all medical records that may be in file.

This Waiver gives my full and legal permission to release my present identity and contact information as shown below and this letter is to remain in effect unless and until formally revoked by me in writing.

Please acknowledge receipt of my Waiver of Confidentiality in writing for my record.

Thank you,

_____
(Signature)

_____
(Printed Name in Full)

_____
(Current Address)

_____
(Current Phone Number)

(11) WAIVER OF CONFIDENTIALITY for SIBLINGS
(California)

STATE OF CALIFORNIA – HEALTH AND HUMAN SERVICES AGENCY   CALIFORNIA DEPARTMENT OF SOCIAL SERVICES

WAIVER OF RIGHTS TO CONFIDENTIALITY FOR SIBLINGS

INSTRUCTIONS:

1. Please complete entire form.

2. **This form must be witnessed by a representative of the California Department of Social Services (CDSS) or a California (CA) adoption agency licensed by the CDSS, or notarized by a Notary Public.*** If the signing of this form is witnessed by the CDSS or a California licensed adoption agency representative, photo identification of the person signing must be obtained and noted on this form. **THIS FORM WILL BE RETURNED TO YOU IF IT IS NOT WITNESSED OR NOTARIZED.**

3. The waiver may be sent directly to the CA licensed adoption agency which handled the adoption, if known, or to the CDSS' Central Office: CDSS, Adoptions Support Unit, 744 P Street, M.S. 3-31, Sacramento, CA, 95814. If the adoption was an agency adoption, the waiver will be returned to you with the name and address of the adoption agency that handled the adoption so that you may send it directly to that adoption agency for processing.

DESIGNATE ONE - I AM THE:

☐ ADOPTEE (age 18 or older)

☐ SIBLING (age 18 or older)
Attach copy of birth certificate

☐ STEP-SIBLING (age 18 or older) Attach copy of birth certificate AND copy of marriage certificate or divorce decree for marriage between birth parent and step-parent.

PART A. *To be completed by adoptee/sibling signing consent*

☐ ADULT ADOPTEE:

By signing this form, I voluntarily and knowingly waive my rights to the confidentiality of personal information known or contained in the files of the CDSS or the CA licensed adoption agency and give my consent to the CDSS or the CA licensed adoption agency to disclose my name and address to my sibling so he/she may contact me.

☐ ADULT SIBLING:

By signing this form, I voluntarily and knowingly waive my rights to the confidentiality of personal information known or contained in the files of the CDSS or the CA licensed adoption agency and give my consent to the CDSS or the CA licensed adoption agency to disclose my name and address to my adopted sibling so that he/she may contact me.

I realize that both of the designated persons must sign a Waiver before the CDSS or the CA licensed adoption agency may disclose identifying information and that signing this Waiver does not necessarily ensure that a contact will be made. The sibling must also comply with all other provisions of Family Code Section 9205.

I certify that to the best of my knowledge, I am an adoptee or sibling of an adoptee. I understand that I should keep the CDSS or the CA licensed adoption agency informed of my current name, address, and phone number in writing.

I understand that I have the right to revoke this waiver at any time by notifying the CDSS or the CA licensed adoption agency in writing.

I understand that if the CDSS or the CA licensed adoption agency has not received a Waiver from each designated person, I may file a petition in the Superior Court to appoint a confidential intermediary to search for the other party to attempt to obtain a Waiver.

NAME (PLEASE PRINT)		BIRTHDATE	OTHER NAME(S) BY WHICH ADOPTEE/SIBLING HAS BEEN KNOWN
STREET ADDRESS	CITY	STATE	ZIP CODE	TELEPHONE NUMBER ( )
SIGNATURE		DATE	

PART B. *To be completed by a representative of the CDSS or a CA licensed adoption agency. If Part B or C is completed, do not complete Part D.*

SIGNATURE OF THE CDSS OR A CA LICENSED ADOPTION AGENCY REPRESENTATIVE   DATE   TELEPHONE NUMBER ( )

AGENCY/DEPARTMENT NAME   ADDRESS

IDENTIFICATION OF ADULT ADOPTEE OR ADULT SIBLING (SPECIFY, I.E., DRIVER'S LICENSE, PASSPORT, ETC.)

PART C. ☐ *Check if notarized signature has been previously submitted to the CDSS or a CA licensed adoption agency.*

PART D. *To be completed by a Notary Public ONLY if Part B or C is not completed.*

State of _____)
)
County of _____)

On _____ before me, _____ , a Notary Public,

personally appeared _____ ,proved to me on the basis of satisfactory evidence to be
NAME OF ADULT ADOPTEE/ADOPTEE'S SIBLING

the person whose name is subscribed to the within instrument and acknowledged to me that he/she executed the same in his/her authorized capacity, and that by his/her signature on the instrument the person, or the entity upon behalf of which the person acted, executed the instrument.

I certify under PENALTY OF PERJURY under the laws of the State of California that the foregoing paragraph is true and correct.

WITNESS my hand and official seal.

_____ (Seal)
Signature

*Definition of Notary Public: A Notary Public is a public officer authorized by law to certify documents and to confirm your identity. Notaries may be located at most banks and credit unions or listed in the yellow pages of your local phone directory.

AD 904A (3/08)   **SEE REVERSE SIDE**

(12) CONSENT FOR CONTACT FOR BIRTHPARENT OR ADOPTEE (CALIFORNIA)

STATE OF CALIFORNIA - HEALTH AND HUMAN SERVICES AGENCY — CALIFORNIA DEPARTMENT OF SOCIAL SERVICES

CONSENT FOR CONTACT

Distribution Instructions:
Original: Agency/Department
Copy: Person Signing

1. Please complete both sides of this form.

2. **This form must be witnessed by either a representative of the California Department of Social Services (CDSS) or a California (CA) adoption agency licensed by CDSS, or notarized by a Notary Public.*** If the signing of this form is witnessed by a CDSS or adoption agency representative, photo identification of the person signing must be obtained and noted on this form. **THIS FORM WILL BE RETURNED TO YOU IF IT IS NOT WITNESSED OR NOTARIZED.**

DESIGNATE ONE:
I am the

[ ] Birth Parent

[ ] Adult Adoptee
(age 18 or older)

PART A. *To be completed by person signing consent.*

[ ] **BIRTH PARENT:**

By signing this form, I voluntarily give my consent to the CDSS or licensed adoption agency to disclose my name and address to my adult biological child who was adopted so he/she may contact me.

[ ] **ADULT ADOPTEE:**

By signing this form, I voluntarily give my consent to the CDSS or licensed adoption agency to disclose my name and address to my birth parent(s) so he/she may contact me.

I understand that the CDSS does not provide search services to locate birth parents or adoptees and that these parties must contact CDSS or the licensed adoption agency to request a Consent for Contact (AD 904) form.

I understand that the birth parent(s) and the adoptee must sign a consent before CDSS or the licensed adoption agency may disclose identifying information and that signing this consent does not necessarily ensure that a contact will be made pursuant to Family Code Section 9204. I understand that the law prohibits CDSS or the licensed adoption agency from soliciting, directly or indirectly, the execution of such a consent.

I understand that I should keep the CDSS or the licensed adoption agency informed of my current name and address.

I understand I have the right to rescind this consent at any time by notifying CDSS or the licensed adoption agency in writing.

NAME (PLEASE PRINT)			OTHER NAME(S) BY WHICH I HAVE BEEN KNOWN

STREET ADDRESS	CITY	STATE	ZIP CODE	TELEPHONE NUMBER ( )

SIGNATURE		DATE

PART B. *To be completed by a representative of CDSS or a CA licensed adoption agency. If Part B or C is completed, do not complete Part D.*

SIGNATURE OF CDSS /ADOPTION AGENCY REPRESENTATIVE	DATE	TELEPHONE NUMBER ( )

AGENCY/DEPARTMENT NAME	ADDRESS

IDENTIFICATION OF BIRTH PARENT/ADULT ADOPTEE (SPECIFY, I.E., DRIVER'S LICENSE, PASSPORT, ETC.)

PART C. [ ] *Check if applicable. Notarized signature has been previously submitted to CDSS or a CA licensed adoption agency.*

PART D. *To be completed by a Notary Public ONLY IF Part B or C is not completed.*

COMPLETED BY Notary Public

The Notary Public must staple the Acknowledgement document to this form and sign and date below.

SIGNATURE OF NOTARY	DATE

*Definition of Notary Public: A Notary Public is a public officer authorized by law to certify documents and to confirm your identity. Notaries may be located at most banks and credit unions or listed in the yellow pages of your local phone directory.

(13) INTERNATIONAL SOUNDEX REUNION REGISTRY(ISRR.org)
REGISTRATION FORM, page 1

RN	S.	DOB	FOR OFFICE USE ONLY		I
STAFF			COUNTRY	STATE	Π

Official Registration Form
-- Confidential --

MAIL TO: ISRR, P.O. BOX 371179, LAS VEGAS, NV 89137

COMPLETE BOTH PAGES of this form, use BLACK ink, THEN PRINT, SIGN & MAIL

Please read the guidelines on page 4. This will help you fill out the form correctly.

This registration is my FIRST ENTRY ☐   an UPDATE ☐

I AM THE: ADOPTEE/CHILD ☐   BIRTH PARENT ☐   BIRTH SIBLING ☐   OTHER: (explain)_____

PRESENT NAME:_____   REFERRED BY:_____

ADDRESS:_____CITY:_____STATE:_____ZIP:_____

TELEPHONE NUMBER(S)   HOME: (____) _____-_____   SOCIAL SECURITY #: _____-____-_____

WORK: (____) _____-_____   E-MAIL:_____

Information About the CHILD   MALE ☐   FEMALE ☐

BIRTH DATE (Month/Day/Year)_____ TIME_____ AM ☐ PM ☐ BIRTH WEIGHT_____lb____oz

HOSPITAL (Birth Place)_____ ATTENDING PHYSICIAN (Or Other)_____

CITY OF BIRTH_____COUNTY_____STATE_____COUNTRY_____

NAME GIVEN AT BIRTH_____

NAME GIVEN AT ADOPTION_____

ADOPTIVE PARENTS NAMES_____

BIRTH CERTIFICATE #'s – File #_____Registrar #_____

IF THIS WAS A PLURAL BIRTH (Twins/Triplets, etc.), How many MALES?_____How many FEMALES?_____

Were they separated by adoption? YES ☐   NO ☐   Their Name(s)_____

COURT OF JURISDICTION_____CITY_____STATE_____

ATTORNEY OF RECORD_____DATE OF FINAL DECREE_____

This adoption was -- PRIVATE ☐   BY AN AGENCY ☐   SOCIAL WORKER/INTERMEDIARY_____

NAME OF PLACEMENT AGENCY_____CITY_____STATE_____

INTERNATIONAL SOUNDEX REUNION REGISTRY, Inc.

Information About the BIRTH PARENTS (at time of separation):
Including all info you know is very important. It helps ISRR determine relationships. Please enter everything you have. Update ISRR when you acquire additional data. Get your non-identifying info from state or agency. Click on "Get More Info" at www.isrr.net for guidelines.

	Birth Mother	Birth Father
NAME(S)		
Maiden Name		
Used At time of Birth		
Signed on Relinquishment/Consent		
BIRTH DATE	Age At Birth	Age At Birth
BIRTH PLACE		
MARITAL STATUS		
RELIGION		
EDUCATION		
OCCUPATION		
MILITARY BRANCH		
ANCESTRY		
DESCRIPTION	HEIGHT WEIGHT HAIR EYES	HEIGHT WEIGHT HAIR EYES
OTHER CHILDREN		
PARENT'S NAMES		

REMARKS: (use a separate sheet if needed)

– To help ISRR use contributions wisely, please keep your address, phone numbers & email current and notify ISRR if you are reunited –

I, the undersigned, hereby give my permission to the International Soundex Reunion Registry to release this vital information to the person(s) for whom this search is conducted. I understand this permission is necessary to activate registration, facilitate contact and for verification of identity, and my relationship to that person or persons.

X Signature Required_____ Date_____

ALTERNATIVE ADDRESS AND/OR PHONE_____

"THIS IS YOUR REGISTRY - YOUR CONTRIBUTION IS TAX DEDUCTIBLE"

Registration remains free because of the generosity of those we serve – ISRR is a non-profit 501(c)3 tax exempt corporation

©1993-2009 International Soundex Reunion Registry   WE LOOK FORWARD TO SERVING YOU!

PLEASE PRINT, SIGN AND MAIL THIS FORM TO:
ISRR, P.O. Box 371179, Las Vegas, NV 89137

ISRR will notify you only when a match is made. If you wish confirmation that your form has been received, include a self-addressed stamped envelope with this registration or update. Please do not send anything that requires signatures, or for volunteers to wait in line at the post office. Thank You.

79

REQUEST TO WAIVE COURT FEES (California 2018)

FW-001	Request to Waive Court Fees	CONFIDENTIAL

Clerk stamps date here when form is filed.

If you are getting public benefits, are a low-income person, or do not have enough income to pay for household's basic needs and your court fees, you may use this form to ask the court to waive all or part of your court fees. The court may order you to answer questions about your finances. If the court waives the fees, you may still have to pay later if:
- You cannot give the court proof of your eligibility,
- Your financial situation improves during this case, or
- You settle your civil case for **$10,000** or more. The trial court that waives your fees will have a lien on any such settlement in the amount of the waived fees and costs. The court may also charge you any collection costs.

Fill in court name and street address:

Superior Court of California, County of

(1) Your Information *(person asking the court to waive the fees):*
Name: _____
Street or mailing address: _____
City: _____ State: ___ Zip: _____
Phone number: _____

Fill in case number and name:

Case Number:

(2) Your Job, if you have one *(job title):* _____
Name of employer: _____
Employer's address: _____

Case Name:

(3) Your Lawyer, if you have one *(name, firm or affiliation, address, phone number, and State Bar number):*
_____

a. The lawyer has agreed to advance all or a portion of your fees or costs *(check one):* Yes ☐ No ☐
b. *(If yes, your lawyer must sign here)* Lawyer's signature: _____
   If your lawyer is not providing legal-aid type services based on your low income, you may have to go to a hearing to explain why you are asking the court to waive the fees.

(4) What court's fees or costs are you asking to be waived?
☐ Superior Court (See *Information Sheet on Waiver of Superior Court Fees and Costs* (form FW-001-INFO).)
☐ Supreme Court, Court of Appeal, or Appellate Division of Superior Court (See *Information Sheet on Waiver of Appellate Court Fees* (form APP-015/FW-015-INFO).)

(5) Why are you asking the court to waive your court fees?
a. ☐ I receive *(check all that apply):* ☐ Medi-Cal ☐ Food Stamps ☐ SSI ☐ SSP ☐ County Relief/General Assistance ☐ IHSS (In-Home Supportive Services) ☐ CalWORKS or Tribal TANF (Tribal Temporary Assistance for Needy Families) ☐ CAPI (Cash Assistance Program for Aged, Blind and Disabled)
b. ☐ My gross monthly household income (before deductions for taxes) is less than the amount listed below. *(If you check 5b, you must fill out 7, 8, and 9 on page 2 of this form.)*

Family Size	Family Income	Family Size	Family Income	Family Size	Family Income	
1	$1,215.63	3	$2,061.46	5	$2,907.30	*If more than 6 people at home, add $422.92 for each extra person.*
2	$1,638.55	4	$2,484.38	6	$3,330.21	

c. ☐ I do not have enough income to pay for my household's basic needs *and* the court fees. I ask the court to *(check one):* ☐ waive all court fees ☐ waive some of the court fees ☐ let me make payments over time (Explain): _____ *(If you check 5c, you must fill out page 2.)*

(6) ☐ Check here if you asked the court to waive your court fees for this case in the last six months.
(If your previous request is reasonably available, please attach it to this form and check here:) ☐

I declare under penalty of perjury under the laws of the State of California that the information I have provided on this form and all attachments is true and correct.
Date: _____

▶

Print your name here _____ *Sign here* _____

Judicial Council of California, www.courts.ca.gov
Revised February 20, 2014, Mandatory Form
Government Code, § 68633 Cal. Rules of Court,
rules 3.51, 8.26, and 8.818

Request to Waive Court Fees

FW-001, Page 1 of 2
→

(16) U.S. STATE DEPARTMENT ISSUED APOSTILLE BIRTH CERTIFICATES
(California and Connecticut)

An "apostille" is a form of authentication issued to documents for use in countries that participate in the Hague Convention of 1961. A list of countries that accept apostilles is provided by the U.S. State Department. If the country of intended use does not participate in the Hague Convention, documents being sent to that country can be "authenticated" or "certified." The U.S. Office of the Secretary of State provides apostille and authentication service to U.S. citizens and foreign nationals on documents that will be used overseas. Types of documents include corporate documents such as company bylaws and articles of incorporation, power of attorney, transcripts, letters relating to degrees, marital status, references and job certifications, deeds of assignment distributorship agreements, home studies, **birth certificates** and papers for **adoption** purposes.

(17) HOSPITAL RECORD OF NEWBORN'S FOOTPRINTS with MOTHER'S THUMB AND FINGER PRINTS

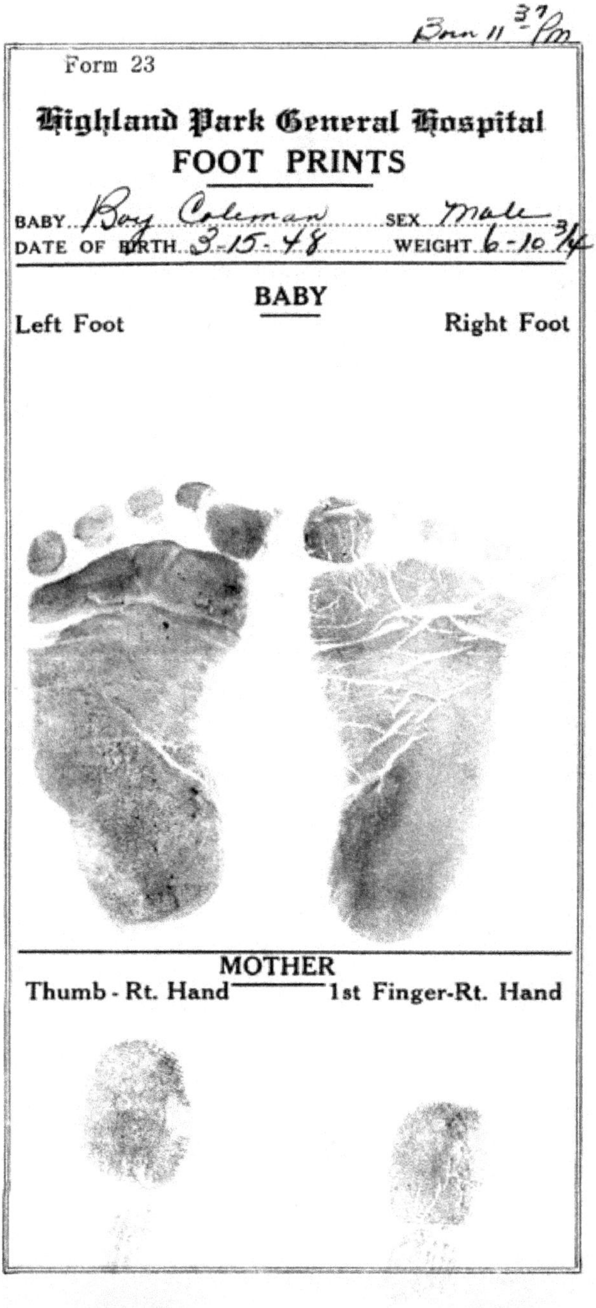

Born 11^{37} Pm

Form 23

Highland Park General Hospital

FOOT PRINTS

BABY Boy Coleman SEX Male

DATE OF BIRTH 3-15-48 WEIGHT 6-10 3/4

BABY

Left Foot Right Foot

MOTHER

Thumb - Rt. Hand 1st Finger-Rt. Hand

(18) CERTIFIED NURSE MIDWIFE (CNM) HOME BIRTH CERTIFICATE & MIDWIFE LICENSE (Illinois)

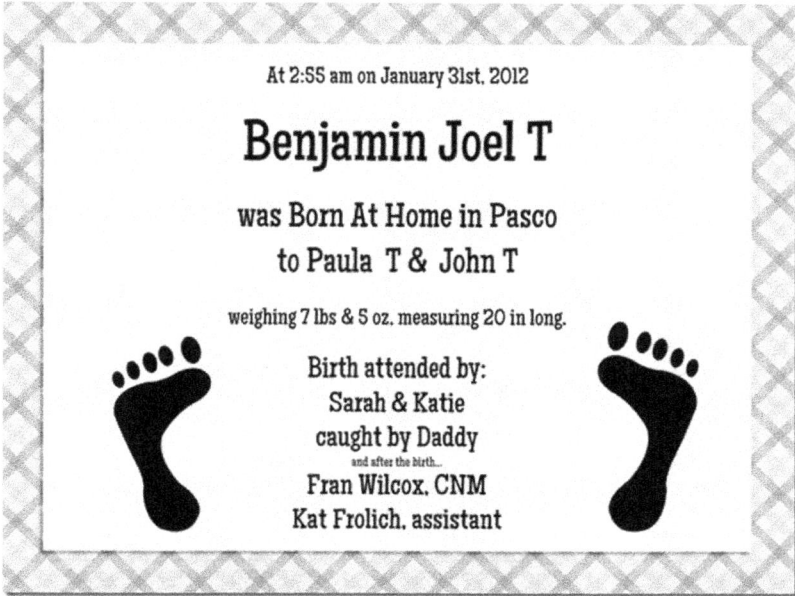

At 2:55 am on January 31st, 2012

Benjamin Joel T

was Born At Home in Pasco
to Paula T & John T

weighing 7 lbs & 5 oz. measuring 20 in long.

Birth attended by:
Sarah & Katie
caught by Daddy
and after the birth...
Fran Wilcox, CNM
Kat Frolich, assistant

NUMBER 1054

STATE OF ILLINOIS

DEPARTMENT OF
REGISTRATION AND EDUCATION

This is to Certify

That *Rudolph N Stone*
is duly registered and entitled to practice as a

LICENSED MIDWIFE

under the provisions of "An Act to revise the law in relation to the practice of the art of treating human ailments"

This License is revocable for the causes specified in the law, and must be conspicuously displayed in the place of business or legal residence of the holder thereof.

In Witness Whereof, the Director of Registration and Education has hereunto affixed his hand and the seal of the said Department this 10th day of May A.D. 1923.

THIS IS A
DUPLICATE
CERTIFICATE

Original License dated August 31, 1916

Attest:

SUPERINTENDENT OF REGISTRATION

(19) COUNTY ISSUED BIRTH CERTIFICATE
(Cook County, Illinois)

The physician or midwife (when in attendance), or the parent or householder should immediately send this certificate securely filled out to the County Clerk of the County in which the birth takes place. Penalty for not making reports within 30 days, fine of $10 to $100, or imprisonment in jail for 30 days, or both.

STATE OF ILLINOIS,

Cook County.

REPORT OF BIRTH.*

VITAL STATISTICS DEPARTMENT—COUNTY CLERK'S OFFICE.

1. † Full Name of Child _____ *Katy Thompson* _____
2. Sex _____ *W* _____ Race or Color (if not of the white race) _____
3. Number of Child of this Mother _____ *2* _____ How many now living (in all) _____ *2* _____
4. Date of this Birth _____ *July 15 – 1913* _____
5. Place of Birth, _____ No. *2645* _____ Street *N. Avers Ave* _____ { City / Village / Town
6. Residence of Mother, _____ No. *Same* _____ Street _____ "
7. Place of Birth

	TOWN	STATE OR COUNTRY	AGE OF
a. Father	*Norway*		*27*
b. Mother	*Ill.*		*24*

8. Full Name of Mother _____ *Dena Thompson* _____
9. Maiden Name of Mother _____ *E. Allgren* _____
10. Full Name of Father _____ *Axel M. Thompson* _____
11. Occupation of Father _____ *Painter* _____
12. Name and Address of Nurse or Attendant (if any) _____ *J McGrory M D* _____ { M. D. or Midwife

Reported by _____ *J McGrory M D* _____ { M. D. or Midwife

Date _____ 19 _____ Residence *8421 Kromel Ave* Telephone *901 B*

* Still-births should be reported on a separate blank form.
† The baptismal or christian name of child should be certified, if possible, when this certificate is made, and should, in any case, be reported to the County Clerk within a year.
‡ In case of more than one child at a birth, a SEPARATE RETURN must be made for each, and the number of each, in order of birth, stated.

(20) CITY ISSUED BIRTH CERTIFICATE
(Chicago, Illinois)

BIRth anD Baptismal certificate

BIRth anD
Baptismal
certificate

Diocese of _Killaloe_   Parish of _Birr_

On examination of the Register of Baptisms of above Parish I certify that

according to it _Thomas_   _Tobin_

was born on _8_ day of _March_ _1863_, and was

baptised according to the Rites of the Catholic Church on_____day of

_____in the Church of _St. Brendans_

Birr by the Rev. _J. Scanlan cc._

Parents _John_ _Tobin_

Ellen _Halloran_

Sponsors _James_ _Keeffe_

Mary _Tobin_

Confirmed_____ Married_____

Signed _Fr. J. Shallow_ _____ P.P_____

Given this _6_ day of _November_ 19 _56_ at _____

Birr

LS.

VERITAS CO. LTD., DUBLIN

86

(22) JEWISH BIRTH CERTIFICATE WITH CHILD'S HEBREW NAME
and CIRCUMCISION CERTIFICATE (New York)

(23) MORMON BIRTH CERTIFICATES-
FROM RECORD AY JUAREZ STAKE, CHIHUAHUA, MEXICO
(Salt Lake City, Utah)

CERTIFICATE OF BIRTH

Church of Jesus Christ of Latter Day Saints

Salt Lake City, Utah, August 3, 1942

This Certifies that according to the Records of the Church of Jesus Christ of Latter Day Saints -

GRANT G. BROWN

was born on the eighteenth day of September, Eighteen Hundred Ninety-nine

at Juarez, Chih., Mexico

Father's name Orson P. Brown

Mother's maiden name Jane Galbraith

Joseph Fielding Smith

Historian of the Church and ex officio Custodian of its Records

(Taken from Juarez Stake, Morelos Ward Record of Children blessed, Book 2118 entry 46). Entered on Records in the year 1899 by O. P. Brown.

(24) "SEX NOT SPECIFIED" BIRTH CERTIFICATE
(Australia)

(25) "3 PARENT" (LGBT) and TRANSGENDER BIRTH CERTIFICATES

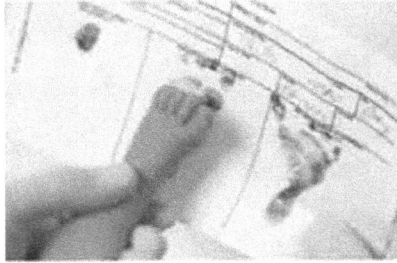

BABY GIRL 'EMMA" HAS 3 PARENTS ON HER BIRTH CERTIFICATE (FLORIDA)

A Miami-Dade (Florida) judge approved a birth certificate listing all 3 of 22-month old "Emma's" parents - 2 women who are a married lesbian couple, and a gay man. This came after a 2-year paternity battle between the couple and their friend who donated his sperm but then wanted a larger role in the girl's life. Her birth certificate now includes the names of the biological father and both women as "parents." At the time, it was regarded as an unusual arrangement and, unfortunately, this modern family wasn't all that happy, since the 3-parent arrangement wasn't what the 2 mothers had in mind. But their attorney, Kenneth Kaplan, explained to Reuters: *"When push came to shove, they figured he would understand the situation. The mistake they made, however, was that there should have been a written document spelling out what his rights and responsibilities were going to be."* Although getting this family together was challenging, the 2 moms now believe they are doing the right thing because they want Emma to "have it all" and believe that inclusion of her biological father, even in some family outings, will be in her best interests. In the end, it's all about love, isn't it? One of the mommies, Cher Filippazzo, says that they believe the best interest for Emma is for her father to have a role in her life. And this author agrees, but also supports returning to *truth* in *all* vital records, including adoptees' birth certificates, still falsified to indicate adoptive parents as the only parents from date of birth and necessitating their sometimes lifelong search for the truth.

TRANSGENDERS CAN CHANGE GENDER ON BIRTH CERTIFICATE (CALIFORNIA)

California Governor Jerry Brown signed a law allowing transgenders to more easily change their birth certificate to reflect the gender with which they may identify later in life. Until now, it was required that a transgender prove they had sex reassignment surgery before they could change the gender on their birth certificate. From now on, they will need only one certification by a doctor stating that they have undergone "clinically appropriate treatment." This Vital Statistics Modernization Act is intended to help transgender people avoid harassment and discrimination in areas such as employment where ID is essential to proving eligibility to work.

DIRECTORY of PUBLIC SOCIAL SERVICES CENTRAL OFFICES and COURTS HOLDING ADOPTION RECORDS - BY STATE

on the following pages are for Requesting Non-Identifying and Identifying Information with Your Waiver of Confidentiality and to determine if a State Registry exists and to be included on it– "Yes" or "No" indicates whether the Court will also release the Adoption Decree (but ask anyhow); Note: Remember, you want the agency and court in the state where the adoption was finalized. Always check online or by phoning to be sure the address is current.

ALABAMA

Family Services
Att: Post Adoption Services
50 Ripley Street
Montgomery, AL 36130
Probate Court – Adoption Decree? Yes

ALASKA

Family and Youth Services
Att: Post Adoption Services
PO Box 110630
Juneau, AK 99802
Superior Court - Adoption Decree? Yes

ARIZONA

Department of Children, Youth and Families
Att: Post Adoption Services
PO Box 6123
Phoenix, AZ 85005
Superior Court – Adoption Decree? Sometimes

ARKANSAS

Children and Family Services
Att: Post Adoption Services
PO Box 1437 (Slot 636)
Little Rock, AR 72203
(501) 682-1569
Probate Court – Adoption Decree? No

CALIFORNIA

Department of Social Services
Adoptions Branch - Att: Post Adoption Services
744 "P" Street – MS 19-73
Sacramento, CA 95814
(916) 324-9084
Superior Court – Adoption Decree? Usually

COLORADO

Department of Social Services
Att: Post Adoption Services
1575 Sherman Avenue
Denver, CO 80203
Juvenile Ct-Denver - Adoption Decree? Sometimes

CONNECTICUT

Department of Children, Youth and Families
Att: Post-Adoption Services
505 Hudson Street
Hartford, CT 06101
(860) 550-6463
Superior Court– Adoption Decree? Sometimes

DELAWARE

Children, Youth and Family Services
Att: Post-Adoption Services
1825 Falkland Road
Wilmington DE 19805
Superior Ct/Orphans Ct – Adoption Decree? Yes

DISTRICT OF COLUMBIA

For Records Since 9/16/56:
Clerk, Superior Court DC Family Division
Att: Post-Adoption Services
500 Indiana Avenue NW
Washington, DC 20001

For Records After 9/16/56:
Clerk, U.S. District Court for District of Columbia
Att: Post-Adoption Services
Washington, DC 20001
Adoption Decree? Always ask.

FLORIDA

Department of Children and Families
Att: Post-Adoption Services
1317 Winewood Boulevard - #7
Tallassee, FL 32399-0700
Circuit Court– Adoption Decree? Sometimes

GEORGIA

Department of Children and Families
Att: Post-Adoption Services
2 Peachtree Street NW - 13th Floor
Atlanta, GA 30308
(404) 657-3438
Superior Court – Adoption Decree? Rarely

HAWAII

Department of Human Services – Adoptions
Att: Post-Adoption Services
800 Richards Street – Suite 400
Honolulu, HI 96813
(808) 586-5704
Family Court– Adoption Decree? Sometimes

IDAHO

Division of Family Services – Adoptions
Att: Post-Adoption Services
PO Box 83720
Boise, ID 83720
Magistrate Court – Adoption Decree? Yes

ILLINOIS

Children, Youth and Family Services - Adoption
Att: Post-Adoption Services
406 East Monroe – Sta. 225
Springfield, IL 62706-1498
(217) 524-2422
Circuit Court– Adoption Decree Sometimes

INDIANA

Department of Family, Children, Adoption
Att: Post-Adoption Services
402 West Washington Street
Indianapolis, IN 46204
Superior Court– Adoption Decree? Sometimes

IOWA

Department of Children and Families
Att: Post-Adoption Services
Hoover State Office Building
Des Moines, IA 50319

Probate/Superior/County Courts –
Adoption Decree? Yes
post-6/41 Adoptees need "Good Cause"

KANSAS

Social and Rehabilitation Services (SRS)- Adoptions
Att: Post-Adoption Services
915 DW Harrison – 5th Floor
Topeka, KS 66606
(785) 368-8157
District Court– Adoption Decree? Sometimes

KENTUCKY

Department of Social Services – Adoption
Att: Post-Adoption Services
275 East Man Street – 3C-E
Frankfort, KY 4621
(502) 564-2147
Probate Court– Adoption Decree? Sometimes

LOUISIANA

Department of Social Services – Adoption
Att: Post-Adoption Services
PO Box 3318
Baton Rouge, LA 79801
(225) 342-4006
Circuit Court – Adoption Decree? No

NORTH DAKOTA

Department of Human Services – Adoption
Att: Post-Adoption Services
311 West Saratoga Street
Baltimore ND 21201
(41) 767-7713
Probate Court pre-1953 adoptions–
Adoption Decree? Sometimes

MASSACHUSETTS

Department of Social Services – Adoption
Att: Post-Adoption Services
24 Farnsworth Street
Boston, MA 0210
(617) 727-0900
Domestic Relations Court– Adoption Decree? Yes

MICHIGAN

Family Independence Agency – Adoptions
Att: Post-Adoption Services
PO Box 30037
Lansing, MI 48909
(317) 335-4652
Probate Court – Adoption Decree? Seldom

MINNESOTA

Department of Children's Services– Adoption
Att: Post-Adoption Services
444 Lafayette Road
St. Paul, MN 55155
(651) 297-2711
Probate Court – Adoption Decree? Usually

MISSISSIPPI

Department of Human Services – Adoption
PO Box 352
Jackson, MS 39205
(601) 359-4996
Chancery Court – Adoption Decree? No

MISSOURI

Department of Social Services – Adoption
Att: Post-Adoption Services
PO Box 88
Jefferson City, MO 65103
Circuit Court – Adoption Decree? Ask

MONTANA

Family Services – Adoptions
Att: Post-Adoption Services
PO Box 8005
Helena, MT 59604
(406) 444-1675
District Tribal Court– Adoption Decree? No

NEBRASKA

Department of Social Services – Adoption
Att: Pos-Adoption Services
PO Box 95044
Lincoln, NE 68509
(402) 471-9333
County Court – Adoption Decree? No

NEVADA

Dept. of Child and Family Services – Adoption
Att: Post Adoption Services
711 East 5th Street
Carson City, NV 89701
(775) 684-4450
District Ct – Adoption Decree? Sometimes

NEW HAMPSHIRE

Department of Children, Families, Adoption
Att: Post-Adoption Services
129 Pleasant Street
Concord, NH 03301
(603) 271-4711
Probate Court – Adoption Decree? Usually

NEW JERSEY

Department of Youth and Family Services- Adoption
Att: Post-Adoption Services
PO Box 717
Trenton, NJ 08625-0717
(609) 984-2380
Surrogates/Domestic Court– Adoption Decree? Seldom

NEW MEXICO

Department of Social Services – Adoption
Att: Post-Adoption Services
PO Drawer 5160
Santa Fe, NM 87502
(505) 827-8416

NEW YORK

Child and Family Services – Adoption
Att: Post-Adoption Services
40 N. Pearl St, Riverview Circle – 6th Floor
Albany, NY 12243
(518) 474-9465
Surrogate/Supreme/Family Courts –
Adoption Decree? Never

NORTH CAROLINA

Department of Social Services – Adoption
Att: Post Adoption Services
325 N. Salisbury – 2401 Mail Service Center
Raleigh, NC 27603
(919) 773-4622
Superior Court – Adoption Decree? Always

NORTH DAKOTA

Children and Family Services – Adoption
Att: Post-Adoption Services
600 East Boulevard Avenue
Bismarck, ND 58505
District Probate Court – Adoption Decree? Ask

OHIO

Family Services – Adoption
Att: Post-Adoption Services
55 East State Street – 5th Floor
Columbus, OH 43266
Probate Court – Adoption Decree? Usually

OKLAHOMA

Dept of Child, Family Services – Adoption
Att: Post-Adoption Services
907 South Detroit – Suite 75
Tulsa, OK 74120
(918) 592-9149
Children's District Court – Adoption Decree? Always

NEBRASKA

Dept of Child & Family Services– Adoption
Att: Post-Adoption Services
500 Summer Street NE – 2nd Floor
Salem, OR 97310-1017
District Court – Adoption Decree? Usually

PENNSYLVANIA

Dept of Children,Youth, Families – Adoption
Att: Post-Adoption Services
PO Box 2675
Harrisburg, PA 17105
(717) 783-7376
Common Pleas Court– Adoption Decree? Never

RHODE ISLAND

Dept of Children and Families – Adoption
Att: Post-Adoption Services
101 Friendship Street
Providence, RI 02908
(401) 528-3605
Probate, Family Court– Adopt Decree? Seldom

SOUTH CAROLINA

Department of Youth Services – Adoption
Att: Post-Adoption Services
PO Box 1520
Columbia, SC 29202-1520
(803) 898-7524
Family Court – Adoption Decree? Usually

SOUTH DAKOTA

Department of Social Services – Adoption
Att: Post Adoption Services
700 Governor Drive – Kneip Building
Pierre, SD 57501-2291
(601) 773-3227
Circuit Court – Adoption Decree? Yes

TENNESSEE

Dept of Children's Services – Adoption
436 Sixth Avenue North
Nashville, TN 37243-1290
(615) 741-9206
Pre-1950 adoptions: Probate Court;
Post-1950: Chancery Ct;
Adopt Decree? Usually

TEXAS

Dept of Protective Services – Adoption
Att: Post-Adoption Services
PO Box 149030 (E-558)
Austin TX 78714-9030
(512) 438-3412
Chancery/District/Circuit Courts –
Adoption Decree? Usually

UTAH

Department of Social Services – Adoption
Att: Post-Adoption Services
120 North 200th West / PO Box 45500
Salt Lake City, UT 84103
(801) 538-4398
Probate Court – Adoption Decree? Never

VERMONT

Dept. of Social/Rehabilitative Services- Adoption
Att: Post-Adoption Services
103 South Main Street
Waterbury, VT 05671
(802) 241-2259
Probate Court – Adoption Decree? Rarely

VIRGINIA

Division of Social Services – Adoption
Att: Post-Adoption Services
700 East Broad Street
Richmond, VA 23219
(804) 692-1872
Circuit Court – Adoption Decree? Usually

WASHINGTON

Department of Children's Services – Adoption
Att: Post-Adoption Services
PO Box 45710
Olympia, WA 902-7986
Superior Court – Adoption Decree? Always

WEST VIRGINIA

Department of Social Services – Adoption
350 Capitol Street – Room 691
Charleston, WV 25330
(304) 558-6444
Juvenile/Circuit Court– Adoption Decree? Usually

WISCONSIN

Department of Child and Family Services – Adoption
Att: Post-Adoption Services
PO Box 8916
Madison, WI 53708-8916
(608) 266-2860
Probate Court – Adoption Decree? Never

VITAL RECORDS ONLINE, BY STATE

Search indexed vital records online or browse actual digitized images of certificates of birth, death and marriage online. This listing directs you to vital records online for the United States, organized by state. The majority of these online vital records can be accessed for free. Those that require a fee to search or view are clearly indicated.

Alabama

- Alabama Death Records, 1908-1974 *Free*
  A free name index to death certificates from the state of Alabama. Extracted information includes (where available) full birth and death date, place of birth and death, parents' names, spouses' name and occupation.

Arizona

- Arizona Genealogy Birth and Death Certificates, 1844-1964 *Free*
  Search public birth certificates (1855-1933) and public death certificates (1844-1958) from the state of Arizona. This free vital records resource from Arizona Department of Health Services includes PDF images of the actual certificates.
- Western States Marriage Records Index *Free*
- http://abish.byui.edu/specialCollections/westernstates/search.cfm
  This growing database includes names and other information extracted from mostly pre-1900 marriage records in several western states, including quite a few from Arizona. More recent marriage records (as late as 1950s) are also included for several Arizona counties.

California

- Western States Marriage Records Index *Free*
- http://abish.byui.edu/specialCollections/westernstates/search.cfm
  This growing database includes names and other information extracted from mostly pre-1900 marriage records in several western states, including California - most notably the counties of Kern, Santa Barbara and Santa Clara. More recent marriage records are also included for several California counties.

Colorado

- Western States Marriage Records Index *Free*
- http://abish.byui.edu/specialCollections/westernstates/search.cfm
  This growing database includes names and other information extracted from 19th and 20th century marriage records in several western states, including a little over 5,000 records from Colorado. The majority of the included Colorado records are from Gilpin and Douglas counties.

Delaware

- Delaware State Birth Records, 1861-1908 *Free*
  Searchable name index and images of Delaware birth records, including delayed birth records, free from FamilySearch.org.

Florida

- Florida Deaths, 1877-1939 *Free*
- Freehttps://www.bocahistory.org/
- name index of Florida death records created by Florida Department of Health and Vital Statistics. Extracted information in this database includes (where available) full birth and death date, place of birth and death, parents' names, spouses' name, occupation, and date and place of burial.

Georgia

- Georgia Death Records, 1914-1927 *Free*
- http://neptune3.galib.uga.edu/ssp/cgi-bin/ftaccess.cgi?_id=7f000001&dbs=ZLGN
  The Georgia State Archives has online digitized copies of death certificates issued by the state of Georgia between 1919 and 1927. There are also a number of certificates from 1914-1918, with the bulk dating from 1917 and 1918.

Idaho

- Idaho Death Certificates, 1911-1937 *Free*
- http://nupepa.org/gsdl2.5/cgi-bin/nupepa?a=p&p=about&l=en
  Free name index to death certificates from the state of Idaho includes most information found on the original certificates including (where available) full birth and death date, place of birth and death, parents' names, spouses' name, occupation, and date and place of burial. From FamilySearch.org

- Western States Marriage Records Index *Free*
- http://abish.byui.edu/specialCollections/westernstates/search.cfm
  This growing database includes names and other information extracted from 19th and 20th century marriage records in several western states, including over 180,000 marriage records from the state of Idaho.

Illinois

- Cook County Birth Certificates, 1878-1922 *Free*
  FamilySearch.org offers indexes and images of certificates of birth as recorded at Cook County, Illinois - including the City of Chicago. Collection still being digitized and placed online and currently includes only years 1878-1915.
- Cook County Birth Registers, 1871-1915 *Free*
  Name index and images of birth registers as recorded at Cook County, Illinois - including the City of Chicago, online at FamilySearch.org. Collection currently includes years 1871-1879, 1906-June 1907, and July 1908-1915.
- Cook County Marriage Records, 1871-1920 *Free*
  Search or browse name index and images of marriage licenses and returns recorded in Cook County, Illinois, including the City of Chicago, online at FamilySearch.org
- Illinois Statewide Marriage Index, 1763-1900 *Free*
  The Illinois State Archives and the Illinois State Genealogical Society offer this free searchable index online. Available information includes the full name of both parties, date and county of marriage, and the Vol. and page number, and/or the license number for the marriage record.
- Cook County Clerk's Office - Birth Certificates, Marriage Licenses and Death Certificates
  Search is free. Payment required to view digital certificates.
  The Cook County Clerk's Office hosts this pay-per-view Web site to access their birth certificates (75 years or older), marriage licenses (50 years or older) and death certificates (20 years or older). Searches are free. Payment is required to view digital copies of the actual certificates. Covers Cook County and the City of Chicago.

Indiana

- Indiana Marriages, 1911-1959 *Free*
  Indexed in partnership with the Indiana Genealogical Society, this free online name index includes details taken from marriage returns and licenses for the counties of Adams, Blackford, Decatur, Franklin, Henry, Huntington, Owen, Rush, and Sullivan.

Kentucky

- Kentucky Death Certificates and Records, 1852-1953 *Paid Ancestry.com subscription required*
- http://kyvitals.com/cgi-sys/suspendedpage.cgi
  This Ancestry.com collection includes the Kentucky Death Index 1911-2000, plus digitized Kentucky death certificates from 1911-1953. Earlier death records including mortuary records, registers of death and return of death are also available for many counties.
- Kentucky Birth Index 1911-1999 *Paid Ancestry.com subscription required*
  https://search.ancestry.com/search/db.aspx?dbid=8788&cj=1&o_xid=0000584978&o_lid=0000584978
  An index to births recorded in the U.S. state of Kentucky between 1911 and 1999, including the following information: name, gender, race, birth date, birthplace, and parents' names.
- Kentucky Marriage Index 1973-1999 *Free*
- http://ukcc.uky.edu/vitalrec/
  An index to about 2.3 million individuals who were married in Kentucky between 1973 and 1999 from the University of Kentucky. Also included are a Kentucky Death Index 1911-1992 and Kentucky Divorce Index 1973-1993
- Kentucky Vital Records Project *Free*
- http://kyvitals.com/cgi-sys/suspendedpage.cgi
  This free resource includes the statewide Kentucky Death Index, plus approximately 250,000 digitized Kentucky death certificates from the twentieth century.

Louisiana

- Louisiana Deaths, 1850-1875; 1894-1954 *Free*
  This free name index to Louisiana Deaths from FamilySearch.org includes statewide death records for all parishes for 1911-1954. Earlier death records available only for Jefferson Parish, 1850-1875 and 1905-1921.

Maine

- Maine Marriage Index *Free*
  The Maine State Archives features this searchable online Marriage Index covering the years 1892 to 1996.
- Maine Death Index *Free*
  A searchable online Death Index covering the years 1960 to 1996 from the Maine State Archives.

Massachusetts

- Massachusetts Death Records, 1841-1915 *Free*
  A free name index and digitized images of Massachusetts statewide death registers and certificates from FamilySearch.org
- Massachusetts Vital Records, 1841-1910 *Requires paid membership to NEHGS*
- https://www.americanancestors.org/databases/massachusetts-vital-records-
  A name index and digitized images of Massachusetts statewide birth, death and marriage registers and certificates from the New England Historic Genealogical Society (NEHGS). Not all record images yet online, but those that are not can be ordered from NEHGS for a small fee.
- Massachusetts Vital Records, 1911-1915 *Requires paid membership to NEHGS*
- https://www.americanancestors.org/databases/massachusetts-vital-records-1911-1915/about?filterQuery=page:5
  A name index and digitized images of Massachusetts statewide birth, death and marriage registers and certificates from the New England Historic Genealogical Society (NEHGS). Births currently completed, marriages complete through 1914 and deaths still to be added in the future.

Michigan

- Michigan Death Records, 1897-1920 *Free*
- http://seekingmichigan.org/discover/death-records-1897-1920
  The *Seeking Michigan* collection from the Library of Michigan features nearly 1 million digital images of death certificates online for free searching and viewing. Use the "Search Digital Archive" box at the top of this page to search this and other Seeking Michigan collections.
- Michigan Deaths, 1867-1897 *Free*
  A free name index and digitized images of Michigan statewide death registration entries from FamilySearch.org
- Michigan Births, 1867-1902 *Free*
  A free name index and digitized images of Michigan statewide birth registration entries from FamilySearch.org
- Michigan Marriages, 1867-1902 *Free*
  A free name index and digitized images of marriages recorded in the state of Michigan from FamilySearch.org

Minnesota

- Minnesota Death Certificates Index *Free*
- http://www.mnhs.org/search/about
  The Minnesota Historical Society has a great online index to Minnesota death records from death cards from 1904 to 1907 and death certificates from 1908 to 2001.
- Minnesota Birth Certificates Index *Free*
- http://www.mnhs.org/search/about
  A free index to Minnesota birth records from 1900-1934, and selected records from pre-1900 from the Minnesota Historical Society.
- Minnesota Official Marriage System *Free*
  Free searchable index to marriage certificates from 87 participating Minnesota counties. Most marriage records date back to the 1860s, although some counties have them back to the early 1800s. Index links take you to an easy order form for purchasing a copy of the marriage certificate.

Missouri

- Missouri Death Certificates, 1910-1958 *Free*
- https://s1.sos.mo.gov/records/Archives/ArchivesMvc/DeathCertificates
  The Missouri State Archives steps up with this free index and digital images to statewide Missouri death certificates from 1910-1958.

New Hampshire

- New Hampshire Birth Records, Early to 1900 *Free*
  FamilySearch.org has online a free index and digital images of early New Hampshire birth records to 1900.

New Mexico

- New Mexico Death Records, 1889-1945 *Free*
  FamilySearch.org has online a free name index to death certificates and records of death from the state of New Mexico. Available information (where provided) includes full name, date and place of birth and death, spouse and/or parents' names, occupation and date/place of burial.

North Carolina

- North Carolina Deaths, 1906-1930 *Free*
  FamilySearch.org features a free name index and digital images of death certificates recorded in the state of North Carolina

Ohio

- Ohio Deaths, 1908-1953 *Free*
  A free name index and digital images of Ohio statewide death certificates from FamilySearch.org

Pennsylvania

- Philadelphia City Death Certificates, 1803-1915 *Free*
  This free online collection from FamilySearch.org includes a variety of digitized death records, depending on the time period: death certificates, returns of death, and even undertaker transit permits.
- Philadelphia Marriage Indexes, 1885-1951 *Free*
  Digital marriage indexes online at FamilySearch.org are arranged by the names of brides and grooms with the year of marriage and license number. Fully searchable.

Rhode Island

- Rhode Island Births & Christenings, 1600–1914 *Free*
- https://www.familysearch.org/search/collection/list
  A partial name index to birth, baptism, and christening records from Rhode Island, compiled from a variety of sources. FamilySearch.org offers coverage details, including how many records are included by location and time period.
- Rhode Island Deaths & Burials, 1802–1950 *Free*
- https://www.familysearch.org/search/collection/list
  A partial name index to death and burial records from the state of Rhode Island. Most of the records extracted in this database of 840,000+ names include source information. FamilySearch.org includes information on coverage details in this article, with details on included records by time period and locality.
- Rhode Island Marriages, 1724–1916 *Free*
  https://www.familysearch.org/search/collection/list
  A partial name index to birth, baptism, and christening records from Rhode Island, compiled from a variety of sources. Scroll down in this article on FamilySearch.org for coverage details, including how many records are included by location and time period.

South Carolina

- South Carolina Deaths, 1915–1943
- https://www.familysearch.org/search/collection/list
  FamilySearch hosts this free online collection of digitized S.C. death certificates from the South Carolina Department of Archives and History. Records are arranged by year and alphabetically by locality, and a searchable name index is also available.
- South Carolina Death Records, 1822–1955 *Paid Ancestry.com subscription required*
  This searchable database plus digital images includes statewide death certificates, 1915-1955; Charleston City death records, 1821-1914; Spartanburg City death records, 1895-1897 and 1903-1914; and Union City death records, 1900 and 1913-1914.
- South Carolina Delayed Births, 1766–1900 *Paid Ancestry.com subscription required*
  https://search.ancestry.com/search/db.aspx?dbid=1239
- This partial database of delayed South Carolina birth certificates (includes digitized images) contains approximately 25,000 birth returns for the city of Charleston, South Carolina from the years 1877-1901, and approximately 55,000 delayed applications for birth certificates from throughout the state, covering the years 1766-1900.

South Dakota

- South Dakota Birth Records Over 100 Years Old *Free*
  More than 225,000 South Dakota births are searchable in this free online database of birth records from the South Dakota Department of Health, including many delayed birth certificates issued for people born before statewide registration began in 1905.
- South Dakota Death Index, 1905–1955 *Paid Ancestry.com subscription required*
- https://search.ancestry.com/search/db.aspx?dbid=8659
  This index to deaths that occurred in South Dakota between 1905 and 1955 contains the death certificate number, name of deceased, county or county code, and date of death.

Tennessee

- Tennessee Death Records, 1914–1955 *Free*
- https://www.familysearch.org/search/collection/list
  FamilySearch hosts this free searchable database, plus digitized images, of Tennessee death certificates from the beginning of statewide registration in 1914.
- Tennessee County Marriages, 1790–1950 *Free*
- Searhttps://www.familysearch.org/search/collection/list and/or browse images of marriage registers, marriage licenses, marriage bonds, and marriage certificates acquired from local Tennessee county courthouses. This growing collection on FamilySearch.org may not yet complete -- browse the records to see what is currently available by county.

Texas

- <u>Texas Deaths, 1890–1976</u> *Free*
- <u>https://www.familysearch.org/search/collection/list</u>
  Almost 9 million digitized records are included in this free collection of Texas statewide death certificates—including delayed certificates, foreign deaths, and probate obituaries—from the Texas Department of State Health Services in Austin, and hosted online by FamilySearch.org.
- <u>Texas Deaths, 1977–1986</u> *Free*
- <u>https://www.familysearch.org/search/collection/list</u>
  Images of Texas statewide death certificates, including delayed certificates, are available online in this free FamilySearch.org collection, from the Texas Department of State Health Services. For a list of records by dates and localities currently published in this collection, select the "browse" feature.

Utah

- <u>Utah Death Certificate Index, 1904–1961</u> *Free*
- <u>https://archives.utah.gov/research/indexes/20842.htm</u>
  The Utah Division of Archives & Records Service hosts free downloadable images of Utah death certificates for the period 1904 to 1960; 1961 is also available as browsable images, but not yet indexed.
- <u>Salt Lake County Death Records, 1908-1949</u> *Free*
- <u>https://www.familysearch.org/search/collection/list</u>
  A free name index and images for Salt Lake County death records from 1908-1949 from FamilySearch. Also included are a few deaths occurring before 1908 where the remains were re-interred between 1908 and 1949.
- <u>Utah Death Registers, 1847–1966</u> *Paid Ancestry.com subscription required.*
  <u>https://search.ancestry.com/search/db.aspx?dbid=6967</u>
  This collection of images and index includes deaths that occurred in Utah between 1905 and 1951, Utah death registers for 1898–1905 (the dates vary slightly by county, and Grand County includes records for 1961–1966), and interment records for Salt Lake City, 1848–1933.

Vermont

- Vermont Vital Records, 1760–1954 *Free*
- https://www.familysearch.org/search/collection/list
  Name index and images (index cards) of town clerk transcriptions of births, marriages and deaths in Vermont through 1954. Indexing is ongoing, and additional records from 1955–2008 will be added to the collection as they are completed.
- Vermont Death Records, 1909-2008 *Paid Ancestry.com subscription required*
- Nahttps://search.ancestry.com/search/db.aspx?dbid=1607me index and images of death certificates and amended death certificates issued in Vermont from 1955–2008.

Virginia

- Death Indexing - Virginia *Free*
- http://lva1.hosted.exlibrisgroup.com/F/?func=file&file_name=find-b-clas29&local_base=clas29 A fully-searchable index to Virginia city and county death registers compiled 1853-1896, part of an on-going project sponsored by the Virginia Genealogical Society. Fifteen cities and counties have been indexed to date.
- Virginia Births and Christenings, 1853-1917 *Free*
- http://lva1.hosted.exlibrisgroup.com/F/?func=file&file_name=find-b-clas29&local_base=clas29
  Almost 2 million names can be searched in this name index to birth, baptism and christening records from the state of Virginia. Online at FamilySearch.org.

Washington

- Washington State Archives - Birth Records, 1891–1907 *Free*
- https://www.digitalarchives.wa.gov/Collections#RSID:5
  Washington State Archives has begun to digitize the birth records in their collections and make them available online, free. (after 1907 are not open to the public) for most counties.
- Washington State Archives - Death Records, 1891–1907 *Free*
- https://www.digitalarchives.wa.gov/Collections#RSID:4
  The Washington State Archives has begun to digitize the available death records in their collections and put them online for free. Available death records cover the period 1891–1907. Post-1907 death records in Washington are not open to the public for research.
- Washington State Archives - Marriage Records, 1866-2002 *Free*
  https://www.digitalarchives.wa.gov/Collections#RSID:4
  These online marriage records include indexed, digitized images created by the Washington State Archives in a project to make the entire marriage series available from the beginning of marriage record keeping in 1866. The more current index records (approximately 1995 forward) are updated by partner Auditors on a periodic basis and may not include images.

West Virginia

- West Virginia Vital Records Research Project *Free*
- http://www.wvculture.org/vrr/
- One of the first states to start making vital records available online, West Virginia hosts indexes and images to birth and death records dating back to about 1853, and marriage records dating back to county formations. Records and time periods available vary by county.

Wisconsin

- Wisconsin Genealogy Index *Free*
- https://www.wisconsinhistory.org/Records/Article/CS15307 Search for pre-1907 Vital Records, including birth, death, and marriage records, in this free online database of the Wisconsin Historical Society.

Wyoming

- Wyoming Marriages, 1877-1920 *Free*
- https://www.familysearch.org/search/collection/list
- A free name index to approximately 14,000 marriage records

DIRECTORY of ADOPTION SEARCH and SUPPORT GROUPS
by STATE (and Canada)

The individuals and groups listed on the following pages, by state, as well as others you may find on Facebook, may provide either support or search assistance, or both, *with or without fee or for "expenses only*," (as with **"Search Angels"** on Facebook), for adoptees or birthparents, depending on what you feel ready to accomplish, how quickly and affordably. You may wish to obtain more information before deciding whether to have contact with the person found. But note that no one can deliver your personal message better than you, and it is better to hear what the other person has to say, firsthand, as the true story of one's birth and adoption is often quite different than what may be in a file folder at Social Services, at a private adoption agency, a lawyer's office, or court file. And most adoptees and birthparents agree that it is always better to know than to always wonder *"Who are by biological relatives?"* and *Why was I adopted?"* or *"Is my child alive and well?"* Phone or email those listed on the following pages to determine:

- their purpose – search? support? both?
- whether they head a chapter of a nationwide network;
- or whether they are an independent searcher;
- whether they network with, or will refer you to others who specialize in the location you need searched;
- whether they hold meetings, on what days, times and location (and if COVID-19 restrictions may apply),
- whether they require a "membership fee,"
- whether their group includes just adoptees, just birthparents, just adoptive parents, or the entire "triad";
- whether theirs is a passive registry or involved in actively searching;
- whether they charge a "search fee" and how it is calculated; and
- whether they require mutual consent of the person found before providing you with their identity and location and any documentation as proof that the right person is found.

ALABAMA
Birth Parents/Adult Adoptees, Birmingham, AL, Audrey Derevenko, 205.837.7377

ARIZONA
Tucson Adoption Reunion Search & Support, Tucson AZ, Harmony Brown, 520.284.0823
Arizona Adoption Circle, Phoenix, AZ, Colleen Campbell, 602.935.4975, 602.486.3042

ARKANSAS
None

CALIFORNIA
Cameron Park Triad, Rachel, 530-558-5336, Beth, 530-677-5658
Oakland Adoptee, Malcolm, 510-336-9284
Sacramento Triad, Linda, 916.359.6777
Sebastopol Triad, Jerilynn, 707.823.7840
Full Circle Support, Orange County, CA, Delayn Curtis, 714.994.1440
Search-Finders of California, San Jose, CA, kris Dollard, 408-356-6711
Concerned United Birthparents, La Mirada, CA, Mimi Janes
Adoptees Connect, Tustin, CA, 214-502-7031, Tineke Lacy

COLORADO
CUB Support Group, Wheat Ridge, CO, Info Line 303-263-1860

CONNECTICUT
Adoption Healing, West Hartford, MJConklin@aol.com, ATPallone@aol.com

DELAWARE
None

DISTRICT OF COLUMBIA
Concerned United Birthparents, (DC Metro), Chevy Chase, MD, Linda Clausen, 202-966-1640
Adoptee-Birthparent Support (ABSN), MD, VA, DC

FLORIDA
Concerned United Birthparents, Lakeland, FL, Patty Collings, 863.299.0767
Orlando Adoption Network (Prospective and Adoptive Parents), Sanford, FL, M. Scott Beaton

GEORGIA
GA Adoption Reunion Registry, Atlanta, GA, Peggy Rothschild, 404.657.3560
Adult Adoptee Support, Karen Whitehead, 678.827.2111, Kate Murphy, 678.684.0396

HAWAII
Adoption Circle of Hawaii, Honolulu, H, Jan, Rhonda, 808.989.7071

IDAHO
Search-Finders of Idaho, Boise, ID, Lois Wight, 208-375-9803

ILLINOIS
Healing Hearts, Bloomington, IL, Marilyn Strohkirch, 309-820-0230
Adoptees, BP & AP Together.Wheaton/Naperville, Jody Moran, 630.778.0636

INDIANA
Online adoptee support, Sherrie Eldridge, All-adoptee@yahoogroups.com, 317.849.5651

IOWA
None

KANSAS
Adoption Concerns Triangle, Topeka, KS, Marilyn Waugh, 785.235.6122
Adoption Triad Support KC, Overland Park, Carolyn Pooler, 816.505.0328, gapmother@aol.com

KENTUCKY
Southland Christian Church Adoptive Families Support, Lexington, KY, tvascassenno@adelphia.net
KY Transracial Adoption Support, Ktag_leaders@yahoo.com
Adoptees Connect, Lexington, KY, 859-475-8306, Pamela Karanova

LOUISIANA
Independent Searcher/Advisor, Kenner, LA, Linda Woods, 504.443.1012, linrwoods@aol.com
New Orleans Chapter, Metairie, LA, Christy Little
Adoptees Birthrights Committee, Baton Rouge Chapter, Delia Pressler, 225.752.3162

MAINE
OBC for ME Triad Support, Portland, ME, Cathy Robishaw
ASCME, South Portland, ME, Peter Jensen

MARYLAND
Concerned United Birthparents, Chevy Chase, MD, Linda Clausen, 202-966-1640, dcmetrocub@aol.com
The Barker Foundation, Bethesda, MD, Abbe Levine
Adoptiee-Birthparnet Support Network (ABSN), MD, VA, DC

MASSACHUSETTS
Adoption Connection, Peabody, MA, Susan Darke
Adoption Community of New England,Wesborogh, MA, 503-366-6812
Adoptive Families Together / MSPCC, Boston, MA, 617-587-1563
Faith Evangelical Free Church Acton,54 Hosmer St., Kristy Bouley, Deborah Henderlong
Braintree, Jeanne Hardy, Sarah Marcella, Linda Perry
Brookline, Matt Paluszek, Tracy Grondin
Jamaica Plain, Randi Schalet, Lori Baeumler
Roslindale, Michelle Novell, Clare O'Donoghue
Swampscott, Kimberly Ryan, Sandi Santanello
Worcester, Deb Tambeau & Donna Warren
CUB Boston Area, Framingham, MA, Kathy Aghajanian, 508.473.4066

MICHIGAN
Adoption Identity Movement of MI (AIM), Tina Caudill
Bonding by Blood, Unlimited,Vassar, MI, Mary Louise Foess, 989.823.4013
Adoptees Connect, Grand Rapids, MI, 616-581-9272, Melissa K. Nicholson, 616-446-5341
Facebook Group: Adoptees Connect, Grand Rapids, MI, urbancurry@gmail.com

MINNESOTA
Concerned United Birthparents, St Louis Park, MN, Sandy Sperazza
Montevideo Adult Adoptee Support, Carleen Helgeson, 320.226.5793
First Nations Repatriation Institute, Sandra White Hawk, 651-442-4872
Duluth Adoptee Support, Michele Benson
Adopted and Fostered Adults of the African Diaspora, Michelle Johnson, 651-341-9636
MN ADOPT, Minnetonka High School Adoptees, Penelope Needham
Adult Adoptees of Central MN,Nikki Knisley
Reuniting Mnnesota (email support), reunitingminnesota@yahoo.com
Adoptees MN, Penny, 612.616.3139, adopteesmn@gmail.com

MISSISSIPPI
None

MISSOURI
Adoption Triad Support Network KC, Liberty, MO, Carolyn Pooler, 816.505.0328

MONTANA
Adoption Constellation Support, Misssoula, MT, Beth Jaffee, 406.880.3052

NEBRASKA
La Vista, NE, Linda Willson, 402-537-4387
Omaha, NE, Sandy Rolles, 402-397-6394, sandyrolls@cox.net

NEVADA
Adoptees Connect, Las Vegas, NV, Janet Nordine, Pamela Roberta, experiencecourage@gmail.com

NEW HAMPSHIRE
Nashua, NH, Paul Schibbelhute, 603.880.7790
Birthmothers of New Hampshire, Dover, NH

NEW JERSEY
Morristown Post-Adoption Support, Ginny Bayard, 973-884-0120, Ginny_bay@yahoo.com
Judy Foster, 973-455-1268 Jfoster7@optonline.net
Pat Fox, 973-998-0967, Patfox1@aol.com
Jane Nast, 973-267-8698, janenast@aol.com
Birth Parent Support Group, Shea Campbell, 201-226-0300, ext. 301, scampbell@cafsnj.org
Adoptee/Birth Parent Support of Central NJ, Randie Zimmerman, 609-510-7504
Concerned Persons for Adoption, Whippany, NJ, Pat Bennett, 908-273-5694, Paben48@comcast.net
Full Circle Triad Post-Adoption Support, Paramus, NJ, Cindi Addesso, 973-427-4521
NJ Adoption Resource Clearing House (NJARCH), 877-427-2465, warmline@njarch.org
Spanish: lalineacalurosa@njarch.org.
Pamela Slaton, Lumberton, NJ, (also NY expertise), 609-702-7535, pamelaobr@aol.com

NEW MEXICO
Operation Identity, Albuquerque, NM, Connie Martin, 505-281-7227, crmarti@swcp.com
Adoption Support Group of Santa Fe, Randa Phillips, 505-466-3839
Adoptees Connect, Albuquerque, NM, 505-205-3400, Michelle Murphy-Martin

NEW YORK
Adoption Group in the Village NYC, Susan McQuirk, 646-303-8343,
Carol Schaefer, 917 743-4118
Adoption Crossroads, NYC & Congers, NY, Joe Soll, 845-268-0283
Manhattan Birth Parents Group, New York, NY, Tony Dupree, 212-544-7487
Adoptees Connect, Buffalo, NY, 716-474-46-57, Susan Ortiz

NORTH CAROLINA
Adoption Triad Dialogue Support, Greensboro, NC, Francie Portnoy

NORTH DAKOTA
Lutheran Social Services of ND, Fargo, ND, 701-235-7341

OHIO
Adoption Network Cleveland, Linda Bellini, 216 482-2323, 216 325-1000
Ohio Birth Parent Discussion, Columbus, Kate Livingston, 614-668-7390, ohiobirthparents@gmail.com
Ohio Birth Parent Group, Cincinnati, Kate Livingston, 614-668-7390, ohiobirthparents@gmail.com

OKLAHOMA
OK Post-Adoption Support, Tulsa, OK, Samantha Franklin, 918-697-2002, Sfranklin568@yahoo.com

OREGON
Adoption Mosaic, Portland, OR, Nina Yates, 503-752-9982
Concerned United Birthparents, Portland, OR, Coco Brush, 503-477-9974

PENNSYLVANIA
Adoption Education & Family Counseling, Doylestown, PA, Robert Allen Hafetz, 267-337-4548
PA Adoption Connection, Canonsburg, PA, (email support), Sherel Kissell, 724-743-1992
PA Adoption Connection, Fort Hill, PA (online support), Glenda Shay, 814-395-3938
Adoptees Connect, Lancaster, PA, 717-327-9912, Kevin Engle
Facebook: Adoptees Connect- Lancaster, PA

RHODE ISLAND
None

SOUTH CAROLINA
Adoption Search for Life, Anderson, SC, Cynthia Walters, 864-287-4328

SOUTH DAKOTA
Parents of Adopted Children, Parkston, SD, 605-928-3955
DSS Child Protection Services Family Support Online, Sioux Falls, SD, 605-335-2776
Lutheran Social Services of South Dakota, Diane Pillar, SW 1-888-201-5061 x2413
Dede Mogck, SW 1-888-201-5061 x 2351
Parents of Adopted Children, Twin Brooks, SD, 605-432-7887, 605-782-0782
Lynne Banks, 605-759-8478

TENNESSEE
Adoption Support and Preservation, 1-888-848-2727
Birthparent Support Group, Nashville, TN, 615-292-3500, annebyrnf@miriamspromise.org

TEXAS

DFW Triad Support, Dallas, TX, Carol DeMuth, 972-414-3639, dfwtriad@yahoo.com
Tapestry Birthmother Support, Irving, TX, Carol DeMuth, 972-315-9628, tapestry@irvingbible.org
Associated Catholic Charities, Houston, TX, Lillian Salinas, 713-526-4611
Roots and Missing Links, Coppell, TX, Glenda Allen, 972-471-0744, glendalpi@aol.com

UTAH

Birthmother/Adoptee Support, Salt Lake City, UT, Donnie Davis, 801-583-6664, Pdj27@aol.com

VERMONT
None

VIRGINIA
Metro Reunion Registry, (international), Alexandria, VA, Metro.reunionregistry@verizon.net
Adoptee-Birth Parent Support, Alexandria, VA (MD,VA,DC), 301-442-9106, ABSNmail@verizon.net
Coordinators2inc, Richmond, VA, Rebecca Ricardo, 804-354-1881

WASHINGTON
WA Adoption Reunion Movement (WARM), Seattle, WA, 206-767-9510
SW Washington Adoption Support, Vancouver, Darlene Wilson, 360-256-8795, wasearcher@msn.com
Adoptees Connect, 253-670-0212, Toni Sheehan- Blake

WEST VIRGINIA
None

CANADA

National Groups
Canadian Council of Natural Mothers
LINKS Post-Legal Adoption Support
Origins BC
Parent Finders of Canada
Birthmothers of Canada

Quebec
Association de parents pour l'adoption quebecoise
Mouvement Retrouvailles

Office of Refugee Resettlement Helpline for Unaccompanied Migrant Children or Sponsors

800.203.7001 | information@ORRNCC.com

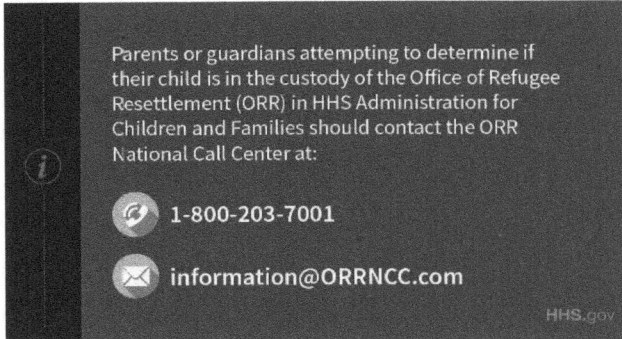

Parents or guardians attempting to determine if their child is in the custody of the Office of Refugee Resettlement (ORR) in HHS Administration for Children and Families should contact the ORR National Call Center at:

1-800-203-7001

information@ORRNCC.com

HHS.gov

How does the ORR National Call Center help parents who are looking for their child?

- The call center collects information from the caller and will send the information in real time regarding the caller's inquiry to the shelter in which the child is located.

- A caller may provide his/her name, contact information, their relationship to the child or child's family, etc.

- The ORR shelter is then responsible for responding to a parent/sponsor/legal representative, after verifying the caller's identity with the child or the child's family in the country of origin.

- The call center does not verify or authenticate relationships, and therefore MAY NOT share the location or other personal information regarding the child with the caller.

Program Contact Information

Office of Refugee Resettlement
Administration for Children and Families
Mary E. Switzer Building
330 C Street, SW
Room 5123
Washington, DC 20201
Phone: 202.401.9246
Fax: 202.401.1022

RESOURCES FOR BLACK MARKET ADOPTEES

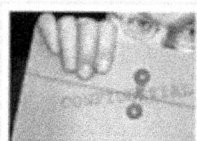

The BABY BROKERS
(Then and Now)

"Gertie's Babies"
(Black Market Adoptees, Montana)

Link for BABIES FOR SALE on eBAY !!
http://cgi.ebay.com/ADOPTION-Website-Business-For-Sale-
ADSENSE_W0QQitemZ380029784359QQ
ihZ025QQcategoryZ46689QQssPageName ZWDVWQQrdZ1QQcmdZViewItem

Baby Brokers are unscrupulous doctors, attorneys, agencies and "humanitarians," including licensed or unlicensed "facilitators" such as clergy, midwives and others. Author of "The Cruelest Con" (http://thecruelestcon.com), Kelly Kiser-Mostrom, warns: "Unethical practices and adoption scams do not only happen to 'adoptive parents.' 'Birth' parents, adoptees and adoption professionals are also at risk. In order for a con to be successful, often the con will hide under the cloak of legitimate professionals." Baby Brokers handle the "Black Market" (illegal) adoptions which may or may not have been legalized in court but usually involve direct payment, or "Gray Market" (questionable) private/independent adoptions in which babies are transferred directly from their parents to would-be adopters and "expenses" are paid. In some states, "baby selling" is not even a crime. The Texas Supreme Court decided only a few years ago that baby selling is "a crime involving moral turpitude... and that attorneys could take advantage of mothers as well as persons adopting" since attorneys routinely represent both parties -- a conflict of interest according to the California Bar Association, yet the

121

practice continues in California's private or independent adoptions (which is 80% of all California adoptions).

Methods of procuring the babies include obtaining signed relinquishments from mothers under duress or coercion, admitting a pregnant woman to a hospital under the name of the adopter or falsely telling the mother "the baby died" shortly after birth and falsifying the original birth record, actual purchase from economically disadvantaged parents in the U.S. and in third world countries and outright kidnapping (see U.S. OK's Child Theft). For the benefit of searching adoptees, the following are known Baby Brokers, both dead and alive -- an ongoing project. Browse AmFOR's search/support pages such as "Search Worldwide, Free", "The Ultimate Search Book", and "Donor Offspring/Parent Registry".

Links to other web-sites will be provided as this page is expanded, and surfing for other web-sites on Internet, using the Baby Broker's name as key-word to search, will also lead to current search/support groups, registries specific to the doctor or institution that handled the birth. Some of these Baby Brokers have been convicted, some were not discovered until long after their deaths, while others still broker babies under protection of current state adoption secrecy laws.

> **NOTE: "If you call the FBI office in the state you were born, they will send you a "Freedom of Information Act" form to fill out to see if they can place you with being a BLACK MARKET baby. This is all new to me. I have been searching for 22 years. I just heard of this. Hoping it will help someone else, too. Much love for your input and helping me. " - Nancy Sharp Strong**

BABY BROKERS DIRECTORY

Estelle Barkan & Unknown Child 1970s

Lisa Mihok & Family 1997, former Barkan Baby kept & abused by Barkan

Katherine M. Cole

Lauryn Galindo

Marianne Gati

Mrs. Ruby Hightower

Ideal Maternity Home Babies

122

The Baby Brokers, by State

Arizona

- **Birth Hope, (see Kurtz, Seymour)**
  See Kurtz, Seymour (on this page) & "Baby Broker Watch: The Facts About
  Seymour Kurtz's Adoption Network," including Easter House at
  http://www.geocities.com/bernw5333/index.html Also Easter House Babies'
  registry is at: http://www.ehbabies.com

- **Burgueno, Attorney Mario Reyes**
  Smuggled Mexican children into the United States for illegal adoptions, in
  conspiracy with a Medford, New York adoption agency run by Arlene Reingold
  and Arlene Liberman. Source: "Motives of Adoption Ring Suspect," 6-2-99 -
  http://www.friends-partners.org/ partners/stop-traffic/1999/0248.htm

- **Reyes, Attorney Mario, (NY-AZ-Mexico)**
  Worked with Arlene Reingold & Arlene Liberman who were partners in a New
  York adoption business. Attorney Mario Reyes (Arizona) handled the adoptions
  of 17 smuggled Mexican children & defrauded Mexican authorities by forging
  documents & having women pose as the biological mothers in illegal adoptions
  for up to $22,000. Source: New York Times, August 4, 2005. See also
  "Adoption Choice" agency in
  http://www.adoptionagencychecklist.com/page673.html

California

- **Doezie, J.**
  Doezie, from Villa Park, CA, pled guilty to recruiting pregnant Hungarian
  women to sell their babies to California couples. Source: LA Times-Orange
  County Edition 3-18-00 - http://www.friends-partners.org/partners/stop-
  traffic/1999/0739.html

- **Gati, Marianne**
  Hungarian-born Canadian/American citizen involved with a California baby selling ring. Source: CNN 6-23-96; Reuters 7-16-96. "Woman Accused of Selling Hungarian Babies": SANTA ANA, California (CNN) -- A Hungarian-born Canadian woman who allegedly brought pregnant women from Hungary to sell their babies in the United States.... Marianne Gati, 48, [was] jailed in California on charges of money laundering, tax fraud, harboring illegal immigrants unlawfully and conspiracy. Gati was arrested ... by federal agents working with the Hungarian National Police to investigate charges that Gati arranged to sell as many as 30 babies in the United States. She promised to pay each mother "$1,000 for a baby with dark features and $12,000 for a baby with light features," according to the complaint. An IRS agent investigating the case said Gati is suspected of turning a $20,000 profit on each adopted baby. Her court-appointed lawyer quoted Gati as saying she ran a legitimate adoption consulting agency." Source: http://www.cnn.com/US/9606/23/newsbriefs/

- **Guzman, Nilda Gierbolini**
  See 11-24-97 excerpted story, "Raised in Peuerto Rico, Crystal Anzaldi To Meet Mother In California" on AmFOR's page at http://AmFOR.net/StolenBabies

- **Kenniker, Dr. Lorraine Eldine, (OB/GYN and adoption facilitator, Santa Barbara, 1960s; died 1972-3)**
  See "Baby Theft 1968?" Link on one alphabetcal list of page links this web page.

- **Leavitt, Attorney David Keene, (U.S. and Canada adoptions)**
  Leavitt was successfully sued for $8-million for conspiring to help a woman give up her child for adoption against the father's wishes. AmFOR intervened in the Kiefer case and in general, with regard to his prectice of soliciting pregnant women via newspaper ads nationwide to come to California where he is licensed to practice, then would advise them to deliver and relinquish their babies in Canada in order to prevent fathers from asserting their claims of parental rights. "The number of American children being adopted by foreign parents is a number that isn�t tracked, according to the U.S. Department of State. However, Canadian immigration statistics show that 600 U.S. born children have been adopted by Canadians since 1995... Experts speculate that the number of children placed abroad is growing; Indianapolis adoption attorney Steven Kirsh placed over 100 American-born children since 1991." Source: The Oregonian, Sunday, July 4, 2004

Colorado

- **Levenhar, Attorney Jeff, (Small Miracles Foundation)**
  Disbarred in 1977 - Source: http://www.geocities.com/shasmith95/

Connecticut

- **Pagano or Pagliano, Mrs., (Midwife-abortionist)**
  Mid-wife who performed abortions in New Haven, CT, late 1930s til arrest in 1938; suspected of black market adoptions; collected fees for "burial" of allegedly "stillborn" babies but there are no birth or death records on these babies, according to one of her victims. Source: Anna & Alfred Carangelo. See

"Baby Theft 1938?" page link, on list of alphabetcial page links on this web page.

Delaware

- **Niles, Dr. Jerome D., ("Niles Babies," Delaware, 1930s-1940s)**

District of Columbia

- **American Friends of Children, (Washington, DC - See also Kurtz, Seymour)**
  See Kurtz, Seymour (on this page) & "Baby Broker Watch: The Facts About Seymour Kurtz's Adoption Network," including Easter House at http://www.geocities.com/bernw5333/index.html Also Easter House Babies' registry is at: http://www.ehbabies.com

Florida

- **Abel, Dr. Bernard, (Jackson Memorial Hospital, Jacksonville)**
- **Barkan, Estelle Katz, (Florida-born babies; facilitated adoptions in Philadelphia, NY, NJ; many finalized in Juarez, Mexico)**
  Estelle was a friend of Helen Tanos Hope and was trained by her. Estelle worked securing Florida-born babies for adoptions in the Philadelphia-New York-New Jersey areas, primarily representing Jewish families. These adoptions followed the same M.O. as Tanos-Hope's, with adoptions often being finalized in Juarez, Mexico. Estelle admits to performing "maybe 70 or 80" of these adoptions, but is suspected of many more as she was active throughout the 1970s. Juarez attorney Vincente Gonzalez Santillan claimed that he finalized adoptions for Barkan and Tanos-Hope at an average rate of one or two per week throughout the 1970s.

  One of Barkan's Babies, Lisa Mihoff (photo above), wrote AmFOR that, for reasons unknown, she and another baby girl were never adopted out. Instead, Lisa states, Barkan kept her and the other girl in Barkan's basement throughout their childhood and abused them physically and emotionally.

  When Estelle was accused of finalizing adoptions in Juarez to make search difficult later, she denied doing it for that reason. She said she did it that way because she was finding babies for people who wanted to be parents, but the legal system at the time would not allow them to be adoptive parents. By way of explanation, Estelle said it was people who were either too old to adopt because back then there were age restrictions, or there was something about their family which would cause them to not be able to pass the home study. At this writing, Estelle is still alive, and, reportedly, when someone calls to inquire about their records, she tells them that she has no records because they were all lost in a move, or a fire, or she never had them, or whatever excuse she chooses. Estelle posed as an attorney, but she was never an attorney as she couldn't pass the bar. Her husband was an attorney, and although they are now estranged, he still practices law. She ran the adoption paperwork through him.

- **Cole, Katherine M., ("Cole Babies"/Cole's Clinic, Miami)**
  Cole Baby Registry is at: http://www.stormpages.com/colebabies/ColeReg2.htm
  Dr. Cole was a "naturopathic physician" in the Miami-Coral Ganles area who allegedly ran an illegal adoption/abortion clinic in her apartment house at 4725 SW 8th Street, Coral Gables, FL, from 1927 to 1963. Young pregnant girls would come to her clinic and leave without their children. The babies were either sold to parents who, for some reason were not able to adopt through normal adoption agencies, or otherwise aborted. The doctor (a.k.a.: Granny Doc) died in 1981 and left no records behind to help us find our real biological parents. Cole delivered thousands of babies between 1927 and 1963 in her clinic in Coral Gables. She housed pregnant girls, delivered their babies and basically sold those babies to couples who were desperate enough to pay her price. She stole the pasts of all those babies by falsifying the information on the birth certificates she signed. Not only did she list adoptive parents as birth parents but also changed dates, even the sex of the babies to prevent her work from being traced. She practiced for decades. Cole was arrested at least 7 times. In 1955 she was questioned in Washington, D.C. in the Kefauver hearings, which focused on black market adoptions. She admitted to "placing" 32 babies. (No records on her placements exist.) Authorities had to know what was happening. Newspapers wrote about her during that time. Her name on a birth certificate coming through the Florida Department of Vital Statistics should have been a red flag. She was arrested 3 times for the illegal abortions that she performed, once for attempted manslaughter, once for unlawful possession of barbiturates, and once for failure to file a birth certificate. She was eventually cleared of all charges except a charge related to an illegal adoption, for which she spent less than a year in jail.

- **Fielding, Lenora, (and husband, Jacksonville)**
  See Michael Chalek's web-site which includes linked AP newsstories on his discovering he had been sold for $200 for black market adoption and his successful efforts to have his adoption annulled - http://ww.adoption-fraud.com - and- http://www.adoption-fraud.com/story.htm

- **Gaylord, Attorney, (private unwed mothers' home)**

- **Hope, Attorney Helen Tanos, ("Children of Hope," Miami area)**

- **Richardson, Mr. and Mrs., (Mt. Dora area)**

- **Suarez, Ephrain, (Suarez Clinic, Miami)**

- **Sutera, Ruby, (Suarez Clinic, Cole's Clinic, Miami)**

- **Thurmond, Rebecca, (Adoption Resources Inc., Coral Springs, FL)**
  Smuggled babies from Costa Rica for U.S. adoptions.

- **Tyre, Dr., (Waterman Hospital, Eustice)**

- **Weathers, Dr., (Jacksonville)**

Georgia

- Hicks, Dr. Thomas Jugarthy, (abortionist, "Hicks Babies," Hicks Clinic, McCaysville)

Illinois

- Baby Farms, (Chicago, 1910s)

- Easter House, Chicago, (5-5-60 to present)
  See Kurtz, Seymour (on this page) & "Baby Broker Watch: The Facts About Seymour Kurtz's Adoption Network," including Easter House at http://www.geocities.com/bernw5333/index.html Also Easter House Babies' registry is at: http://www.ehbabies.com

- Kurtz, Seymour, (procured babies worldwide)
  Used several agencies to procure babies worldwide, many placed via Casa del Sur, Mexico, & Tzyril Foundation in same offices as Easter House (Chicago), which he founded to legalize placements, & communicated availability of babies via Stitching Suzu in The Hague, Holland. Each of the aforementioned entities handled adoptees' "home studies." His Suku Corporation, a Delaware coporation, handled legal & immigration work involved in Mexico adoptions. He also used Friends of Children (Atlanta, Georgia), Birth Hope (Phoenix, Arizona), American Friends of Children (Washington, DC), La Sociedad (Tlaxcala, Mexico). See "Baby Broker Watch: The Facts About Seymour Kurtz's Adoption Network," including Easter House at http://www.geocities.com/bernw5333/index.html. Also Easter House Babies' registry is at: http://www.ehbabies.com

Indiana

- Shapiro, Lydia, (Ft. Wayne)

Kansas

- Glassen, Dr. Mary Townsend, ("Dr. Mary"stole 4,000 babies, most from Miami/N.Kansas)

- Robinson Sr., John Edward, ("Internet Slavemaster" Serial Killer and Baby Broker)
  Killed 6 women over 15 years in Kansas and Missouri, taking the baby daughter of one of them for illegal adoption. In January 1984, Lisa Stasi and her 4-month-old daughter met Robinson while staying at a Kansas City shelter for battered women. While separated from her new husband, Carl, she still kept in touch with his family. She told them that a businessman named John Osborne, later identified as Robinson, had put her up at a local hotel. She also told them he promised to set her up with a job in the Chicago area and, ominously, asked her to sign her name to four pieces of blank stationary. Then she disappeared. The night of Jan. 10, 1985, Robinson hosted a joyous family reunion with his brother and sister-in-law. The childless couple had been trying to adopt a baby for years and Robinson had told them he might be able to help. That morning they flew from their home in the Chicago area to Kansas City, just a day or so after Robinson called to say he had finally found the

perfect baby, a girl. Source: "Kansas v. Robinson: Internet Slavemaster Murder Trial," Court TV, 9-23-02,
http://www.courttv.com/trials/robinson/background.html

Maryland

- **Shrybman, Attorney James A.**
Per Attorney Shrybman's letter request, and as courtesy, AmFOR deleted an old newspaper article about him that has circulated around Internet and that had been on this page for many years, because some of the information, while true at the time of the report, was subsequently revised, and, according to Shrybman, was retracted by the newspaper. The second of Shrybman's letters about the matter was a 4-pager which, like his first letter, included ample legalese to intimidate any layman, and which, in part, opened debate as to his objection to the term "Baby Broker" as it was applied to him on this page. I responded as follows: "With regard to your new objection to the term "Baby Broker," you do state in your letters, and publicly on your own website, that you do *'facilitate'* (i.e. procure, broker) babies for your clients, and that it is a *'business'* (for a fee and assumably to the extent that the law allows), just as a *facilitator* of real estate transactions between Buyer and Seller for a commission is termed a real estate *'broker.'* Some years ago, a Los Angeles Times cover story, *'The Baby Brokers'* featured several adoption attorneys who became prominent as result of their *controversial* practices, just as you state that your 'creative' methods as a *"pioneer"* in your field drew public criticism, both positive and negative, as cited on your own public website. (By the way, we favor 'creative' expressions of custody, such as individualized improved Legal Guardianships, rather than adoption, in *child's* best interests.) Anyhow, one of the attorneys featured in the Times piece (or his attorney, I don't recall which) wrote me demanding, under threat of lawsuit, retraction of the term 'Baby Broker' in my article referencing him per the Times article. I responded that the term 'Baby Broker' is now part of the vernacular for his profession (as for yours and as the Times documents) but also that I would welcome the opportunity of having the issue of brokering babies (human beings) addressed in court. (See Carangelo v. O'Neill, State of CT). I never heard from him or his lawyer again. Also, as you agreed, the truth is not libel...and surely my/AmFOR's opinons and the opinions of thousands of others who posted on AmFOR's site [including on the petition at AbolishAdoption.com], have the right of free speech and opinion ,on such issues as the practice of adoption and surrogacy etc, on such a site devoted to those issues, and cannot be censored just because 'It might upset someone.' " [I would add that the first thing Baby Brokers change is the child's TRUE NAME and BIRTH CERTIFICATE; the second is "allowable" adoption TERMINOLOGY, or as AmFOR calls it, "AdoptSpeak" (See "AdoptSpeak & Censorship" page on this site.)]

Mississippi

- **Balouch, Vickie**
In 2003, Vickie Balouch was convicted in Pikes County, Missippi, for illegally "placing out children" for money, a felony crime in Mississippy.

Montana

- **Pitkanen, Gertrude, (abortionist; "Gertie's Babies," Butte, 1940s)**
  Although not a doctor, Gertrude Pitkanan performed illegal abortions and sold babies in Butte, Montana for 25 years.

Nevada

- **Magelby, Attorney Calvin, (accomplice to Dr. Wallace; Las Vegas, 1950s)**
- **Wallace, Dr. E Basie, (Las Vegas, 1951-1958)**

New York

- **Bernard, Bessie, (A Brooklyn housewife who procured babies from FL, sold in NY and surrounding are)**
- **Butterbox Babies, (see YOUNG, Lila Gladys, Nova Scotia/Canada)**
- **Fenichel, Attorney Seymour, (Child Haven of NE Pennsylvania)**
  Indicted in New York City along with Fenichel's daughter Deborah Fenichel Greenspan and his adopted daughter Harriet Lauer and her husband Lawrence Lauer, on 144 counts including illegally operating Child Haven of Northeastern Pennsylvania, a private adoption agency through which they ran a baby selling scheme that lured pregnant teenagers and bilked 100 couples of $500,000 -- only 50 of the couples actually got babies. Fenichel's Black Market Adoptees are now seeking answers and sharing information via FACEBOOK.
- **Lieberman, Arlene, (NY-AZ-Mexico)**
  Worked with Arlene Reingold as partners in an adoption business & together they worked through Attorney Mario reyes (Arizona), to "legalize" adoptions of 17 smuggled Mexican children and to defraud Mexican authorities by forging documents & havng women pose as the biological mothers in illegal adoptions for up to $22,000. Source: New York Times, August 4, 2005. See also "Adoption Choice" agency in
  http://www.adoptionagencychecklist.com/page673.html
- **Spencer, Attorney Joseph**
- **Springer, Dr., ("Springer Babies," Springer Hospital, Union)**

Ohio

- **Rosen, Dr. Oscar, ("Rosen Babies," Cleveland, 1950s)**

Tennessee

- **Kelley, Judge Camille, (accomplice to Georgia Tann, 1920s-1940s)**
- **Tann, Georgia, (stole 5,000 babies, TN Children's Home Society, Memphis; sold to KY, NY, CA coup)**
  See 3/91 story, "The Woman Who Stole 5,000 Babies" excerpted on AmFOR's page at http://AmFOR.net/StolenBabies

Texas

- **Hightower, Mrs. Ruby, (Texarkana, TX)**
- **Leviton, Attorney Albert**
  Involved in "legalizing" a kidnap & sale for adoption in Dallas. See 10-2-92 excerpted staory, "Years Later Mom Says Stillborn Child Alive" on AmFOR's page at http://AmFOR.net/StolenBabies
- **Salmon, Attorney Robert F., (deceased)**
  See HIGHTOWER, Texarkana, Texas (under TEXAS listings on this page)
- **Thacker, Attorney Leslie Hazlett, (convicted of baby selling)**

Washington

- **Davin, Lynn, (See "Seattle International Adoptions" under "Other Countries")**
- **Galindo, Lauryn, (See "Seattle International Adoptions" under "Other Countries")**
- **Seattle International Adoptions, (See listing under "Other Countries" on this page)**

Wisconsin

- **Adoption Choice (agency), (under ongoing investigation)**
  See http://www.adoptionagencychecklist.com/page673.html

INTERNATIONAL BABY BROKERS
Argentina

Child of Political Prisoners Sues "Adoptive" Parents , AP, BUENOS AIRES, Thursday, Feb 21, 2008, Page 7

A 30-year-old woman is suing her "adoptive" parents for kidnapping in a case that opened in an Argentine court on Tuesday, becoming the first child of disappeared political prisoners to press such charges. Maria Eugenia Sampallo Barragan accused her "adoptive" parents Osvaldo Rivas and Maria Cristina Gomez Pinto of falsifying adoption documents to hide her identity. She made no comments on leaving court on Tuesday.

Thousands of leftists and dissidents vanished after being abducted by security forces during Argentina's 1976 to 1983 military regime, and human rights groups say more than 200 children were taken and given to military or politically connected families to raise.

Sampallo, who in 2001 learned that she is the daughter of missing political prisoners Mirta Mable Barragan and Leonardo Ruben Sampallo, is one of 88 young people who determined their identity with DNA tests coordinated by the human rights group Grandmothers of the Plaza de Mayo. Sampallo's mother was six months pregnant when she and her father were abducted on Dec. 6, 1977, said Sampallo's lawyer, Tomas Ojea Quentin. He said Sampallo was born in February 1978, while her mother was being held at a clandestine torture center.

Ojea Quentin said former army captain Enrich Berthier is facing related baby theft charges in the case. He is being held at a military unit, while Sampallo's "adoptive" parents are reportedly free. Lawyers for Berthier and the Gomez Pintos refused comment when they left the courthouse.

The case marks the first time a woman has taken her "adoptive" parents to court in Argentina. There have been at least three earlier trials involving suspected illegal adoptions dating to the dictatorship that resulted in convictions -- but the plaintiffs were not the adopted children.

Canada

- **Ideal Maternity Home Babies,** (Nova Scotia -- See **Lila and William Young**, and Photo of unidentified babies,) **Rev. Peacock**, (Quebec); **Lila Gladys and William Young**, (Ideal Maternity Home and **"Butterbox Babies,"** Nova Scotia)
  For detailed information on the Youngs and their black market baby brokering in the 1930s-1940s, go to: http://www3.ns.sympatico.ca/bhartlen/PAGE1.HTM

- North American Council on Adoptable Children (See "Other baby Brokers, below)

China

In China, Dark Side of Adoption Exposed
Parents speak out on coercion, theft of babies for profit
by Barbara Demick, LA Times, 9-27-09, excerpted from Boston Globe article at:
http://www.boston.com/news/world/asia/articles/2009/09/27/in_china_dark_side_of_adoption_exposed/

TIANXI, China - ...One day in spring 2004, he presented himself at Yang Shuiying's doorstep and commanded: *"Bring out the baby."* ... *"I'm going to sell the baby for foreign adoption. I can get a lot of money for her,"* he told the sobbing mother as he drove her with the baby to an orphanage in Zhenyuan, a nearby city in the southern province of Guizhou. In return, he promised that the family wouldn't have to pay fines for violating China's one-child policy. Then he warned her: *"Don't tell anyone about it."* ... *"I didn't understand that they didn't have the right to take our babies,"* she said.

...Since the early 1990s, some 80,000 Chinese children have been adopted abroad, the majority going to US families. The conventional wisdom has been that the babies, mostly girls, were abandoned by their parents because of the preference for boys and China's restrictions on family size... Parents who say their children were taken complain that officials were motivated by the $3,000 per child that adoptive parents pay orphanages... The Chinese Center for Adoption Affairs, the government agency that oversees foreign and domestic adoption, rejected repeated requests for comment... For adoptive parents, the possibility that their children were forcibly taken from their birth parents is terrifying. *"When we adopted in 2006, we were fed the same stories, that there were millions of unwanted girls in China, that they would be left on the street to die if we didn't help,"* said Cathy Wagner, an adoptive mother from Nova Scotia. *"I love my*

131

daughter, but if I had any idea my money would cause her to be taken away from another mother who loved her, I never would have adopted."

...Each town has a family planning office, usually staffed by Communist Party cadres who have broad powers to order abortions and sterilizations. People who have additional babies can be fined up to six times their annual income - fines euphemistically called "social service expenditures." *"The family planning people are more powerful than the Ministry of Public Security,"* said Yang Zhizhu, a legal scholar in Beijing. Throughout the countryside, red banners exhort, *"Give birth to fewer babies, plant more trees,"* and, more ominously, *"If you give birth to extra children, your family will be ruined."* ...Once a child is taken to an orphanage, parents can lose all rights. Zhou [Changqi] tried repeatedly over three years to get into the Changsha Social Welfare Institute, one of the major orphanages sending babies abroad, until one day he was told: *"It's too late. Your daughter has already gone to America."*

Guatemala

GUATEMALAN ARMY STOLE CHILDREN FOR ADOPTION, REPORT SAYS

From CNN.com, 9-11-09: "The Guatemalan army stole at least 333 children and sold them for adoption in other countries during the Central American nation's 36-year civil war, a government report has concluded. Many of those children ended up in the United States, as well as Sweden, Italy and France, said the report's author and lead investigator, Marco Tulio Alvarez. In some cases, the report said, parents were killed so the children could be taken and given to government-operated agencies to be adopted abroad. In other instances, the children were abducted without physical harm to the parents." [See PHOTO, above, of **3 out of 4 Galicia family Guatemalan children stolen for adoption & later luckily reunited with their mother, Clara Galicia.**]

Haiti

Haitian born adoptees currently being trafficked by nameless baby brokers for adoptions in the U.S., Canada and France will have a difficult time when they begin searching for answers to "Who am I?" and "Are my parents looking for me?" On 1-7-10, a 7.0 earthquake destroyed Port-au-Prince, Haiti, killing an estimated 200,000 inhabitants and leaving [at least] tens of thousands of children assumed orphaned, in addition to about 380,000 pre-earthquake orphans (estimates are by UNICEF). American would-be adopters, the Catholic Church, international adoption agencies and independent adoption facilitators applied pressure on the Haitian government in order to airlift the alleged orphans before anyone could confirm whether their parents or relatives are still alive -- At this writing, the first 500 or so alleged orphans were airlifted to the U.S. (according to the U.S. State Department)and 900 children were in process of being adopted from Haiti and placed in U.S. homes.

According to The Toronto Star (in "First Haitian Orphans To Arrive Today" by Allan Woods, 1-24-10), "In all, 154 Haitian children were approved in a fast-track adoption process, agreed to by the Canadian and Haitian governments... Officials suspect many orphans, either given up for adoption at birth, or those who lost parents in the earthquake, are being illegally spirited out of their homeland by childless families or organized traffickers [or sexual predators] hoping to profit from Haiti's administrative chaos.... The earthquake brought down the government building that housed all those records; it also killed the judge responsible for giving final approval to adoptions."

It is known that 53 children were airlifted to Pittsburgh (ABC World News, 1-19-10) and Catholic leaders pushed both Haitian and U.S. governments to airlift an unknown number of children to South Miami. At this writing, despite that Haiti has halted adoptions, the kidnap of Haiti's children continues:

Excerpted from Afrikan World News, 1-31-10
"WHITES ARRESTED FOR TRYING TO KIDNAP BLACK CHILDREN IN HAITI"

PORT-AU-PRINCE, Haiti (Jan. 31) -- Ten U.S. Baptists detained trying to take 33 children out of earthquake-shattered Haiti without government permission say they were just trying to do the right thing, applying Christian principles to save Haitian children. But their "Orphan Rescue Mission" is striking nerves in a country that has long suffered from child trafficking and foreign interventions, and where much of the aid is delivered in ways that challenge Haiti's own rich religious traditions. Prime Minister Max Bellerive on Sunday told The Associated Press that the group was arrested and is under judicial investigation "because it is illegal trafficking of children and we won't accept that." The Americans are the first people to be arrested since the Jan 12 quake on such suspicions. No charges have been filed. "From what I know until now, this is a kidnapping case," Bellerive told CNN.

...The government and established child welfare agencies are trying to slow Haitian adoptions amid fears that parentless or lost children are more vulnerable than ever to being seized and sold. Without proper documents and concerted efforts to track down their parents, they could be forever separated from family members able and willing to care for them.
....The church members, most from Idaho, said they were only trying to rescue abandoned and traumatized children....The children, ages 2 months to 12 years old, were taken to an orphanage run by Austrian-based SOS Children's Villages, where spokesman George Willeit said they arrived "very hungry, very thirsty, some dehydrated." One (8-year-old) girl was crying, and saying, 'I am not an orphan. I still have my parents.' And she thought she was going on a summer camp or a boarding school or something like that," Willeit said. The orphanage was working Sunday to reunite the children with their families, joining a concerted effort by the Haitian government, the United Nations, the International Committee of the Red Cross and other NGOs. As the poorest country in the western hemisphere, Haiti is in a difficult spot - it needs aid, but deeply resents foreign meddling. Many have an uneasy relationship with American evangelical Christian groups that funnel hundreds of millions of dollars into their missions in Haiti. Since Haiti became the world's first black republic in 1804, its people have seen several U.S. military occupations, was wrongly blamed for the spread of AIDS and has been vilified for the Voodoo traditions brought from West Africa. Voodoo is one of Haiti's two constitutionally recognized religions, along with

Roman Catholicism, and two-thirds of Haiti's 9 million people are said to worship its spirits. One Voodoo leader said the Idaho group's plan - to give each child "new life in Christ" while facilitating their adoptions by "loving Christian families" in the United States - is deeply offensive. ... We need compassion, not proselytizing now, and we need aid - not just aid going to people of the Christian faith." ...The 10 detained Americans include members of the Central Valley Baptist Church in Meridian, Idaho, and the East Side Baptist Church in Twin Falls, Idaho. They are part of the Southern Baptist Convention, which is America's largest Protestant denomination and has extensive humanitarian programs worldwide.

Mexico

- **Casa del Sur**
  See **KURTZ, SEYMOUR**, under Illinois **La Sociedad**, (Tlaxcala, Mexico); Attorney Mario Reyes, (NY-AZ-Mexico);
  Arlene Reingold & Arlene Liberman were partners in a New York adoption business & worked with Attorny Mario Reyes (Arizona) who handled the adoptions of 17 smuggled Mexican children, & defrauded Mexican authorities by forging documents & having women pose as the biological mothers in illegal adoptions for up to $22,000. Source: New York Times, August 4, 2005. See also **"Adoption Choice"** agency in
  http://www.adoptionagencychecklist.com/page673.html

OTHER BABY BROKERS
(Foreign & Domestic)
BABY BROKERS NOMINATED FOR 2009 "DEMONS OF ADOPTION AWARD"

by Poung Pup Legacy at http://poundpuplegacy.org/node/37652

Each year Pound Pup Legacy presents the "Demons of Adoption Award" to raise a voice against adoption propaganda and the self congratulatory practices of the Congressional Coalition on Adoption Institute's annual Angels in Adoption AwardsTM. The 2009 nominees are:

- **Adoptions First** - for offering of a free birth mothers package;
- **Athanasios Kollias aka Teo** - for the involvement in various Guatemalan child trafficking cases;
- **Barnardos** - for promoting the removal of children and having them adopted as the solution to family breakdown;
- **Bethany Christian Services** - for using coercive tactics obtaining infants for their customers;
- **Deborra Lee-Furness** - for pushing laxer regulations in inter-country adoption;
- **Harry and Bertha Holt** - for starting the placement of "special needs children" who are truly not adoptable, into the homes of already huge families;

- **Independent Adoption Center** - for plugging their business on WE TV's "Adoption Diaries," making them the non-denominational Bethany;
- **Joint Council on International Children's Services** - for supporting temporary movement of foreign children to America because such trial-basis "exchange" programs "help" the adoption process;
- **LDS Family Services** - for using coercive tactics in obtaining infants for adoption and for not respecting paternal rights;
- **Scott and Karen Banks** - for child trafficking, coercive adoption practices and the abandonment of their adopted children;
- **The Dutch Ministry of Justice** - for preventing research into corrupt adoption practices in China, because of diplomatic and business relations with that country;
- **The Malawi Government** - for allowing Madonna to adopt Mercy James
  NOTE: AmFOR would ADD to that list:
- **National Council For Adoption** (NCFA) - NOT a government agency, is the largest lobby of US. adoption agencies using government funds (our tax dollars) allocated via the Safe And Stable Families Amendment ACT (SASFA) as well as private grants to promote closed adoptions
  2005: $297,611,000; 2004: $405,814.000; 2003: $613,703.000; 2002: $400,234,000. and reports $1-million from "public support" plus $50-million in "membership fees."
  On February 16, 2009, President Obama signed the American Recovery and Reinvestment Act of 2009 (ARRA). Among other provisions, the ARRA provides **$187 BILLION** to increase the federal medical assistance percentage (FMAP) for state Medicaid programs **and for Adoption**. NCFA is beating a path to that funding.
  For extensive info on NCFA, go to: "The National Council For Adoption: Mothers, Money, Marketing, and Madness" - by Claudia Corrigan D'Arcy
  http://www.divinecaroline.com/22095/39669-national-council-adoption--mothers--money-

- **North American Council on Adoptable Children** - supports adoption in the U.S. and Canada as public policy, providing catalog-style photos of "adoptable" children, most of whom are on behavior modifying drugs such as Ritalin and Melaril.

- **U.S. Government** - has used $-BILLIONS of our tax dollars to increase adoptions - In addition to over **$19 BILLION awarded to 38 states and Puerto Rico** (Eight states California, Florida, Indiana, Louisiana, Minnesota, North Carolina, Pennsylvania, and Texas) earned more than a million dollars. Florida and Texas earned the highest payments -- $9,754,990 and $4,969,734 respectively. In 2009, $35-million went to increasing, FY-2008 adoptions, **$187-BILLION went to programs including Title IV-E Adoption Assistance)** SEE ALSO "U.S. OK's Baby Theft (includin Pfund Memo) at loricarangelo.com/childtheft.html - **US State Dept. says children kidnapped from other countries can be legally adopted in the United States under state adoption secrecy laws. The U.S. is also the largest market for stolen children in the world, making the federal government the largest Baby Broker in the world.**

INDEX

ABOUT THE AUTHOR

LORI CARANGELO is no stranger to the world of adoption and searching. She searched for and found her own biological son 18 years after he had been adopted, and also found her 2 adult half-sisters who she never knew existed. She then "paid it forward" via her nationwide volunteer network, Americans for Open Records (AmFOR), which, for over 20 years, enabled thousands of adoptees and their birth families to connect without fee. She was a Data Source to the United Nations Rights of the Child, including the "Sale for Adoption Report," and a contributor to the Hague Intercountry Adoption Treaty Conference.

She is retired from 25 years administrative governmental and private sector projects in Santa Barbara and Palm Desert, California, has contributed over 600 published articles on adoption and family rights issues to major newspapers, and authored more than 25 unique non-fiction adoption-themed and true crime books. And there are more to come.

More Books by Lori Carangelo

THE ULTIMATE SEARCH BOOK –Worldwide Edition
Adoption, Genealogy & Other Search Secrets

THE ADOPTION AND DONOR CONCEPTION FACTBOOK
*The Only Comprehensive Source of U.S. & Global Data on the
Invisible Families of Adoption, Foster Care & Donor Conception*

CHOSEN CHILDREN
Children as Commodities in America's Failed Foster Car, Adoption and Immigration Systems

ADOPTION UNCENSORED
4 Decades of Politics, People and Commentary

CARANGELO v. CONNECCTICUT
A Case of Lifelong Opposition to Government Protected Child Stealing

BLOOD RELATIVES
A True Story of Family Secrets and Murders

ESPOSITO
The First Mafioso

KONDRO
The "Uncle Joe" Killer

JAMES MUNRO –
And the Freeway Killers

EYEWITNESS
The Case of the Carefully Crafted Central Coast Rapist

SERIAL KILLERS ON THE INTERSTATE
200 Highway Killers by State

RAGE!
How an Adoption Ignited a Fire

SCHOOL SHOOTERS
Why They Did It and America's War on Guns

ADOPTED KILLERS
430 Adoptees Who Killed – How And Why They Did It

THE 8 BALL CAFÉ
Stories of Adoption, Addiction and Redemption

www.ingramcontent.com/pod-product-compliance
Lightning Source LLC
Chambersburg PA
CBHW071547040426
42452CB00008B/1101